eLeadership

Proven Techniques for Creating

an Environment of Speed and Flexibility

in the Digital Economy

Susan Annunzio

with Julie Liesse

The Free Press

New York   London   Toronto   Sydney   Singapore

*f*P

THE FREE PRESS
A Division of Simon & Schuster, Inc.
1230 Avenue of the Americas
New York, NY 10020

Designed by Katy Riegel

Manufactured in the United States of America

1   3   5   7   9   10   8   6   4   2

Library of Congress Cataloging-in-Publication Data is available

ISBN 0-7432-0438-7

To Christopher and Angie Rose
My soul and my heart

Acknowledgments

I would like to thank the many individuals who have helped make this book possible.

First, the many young people who have taught me how to lead, who challenged my ideas and brought energy, creativity, and joy into my life: I would especially like to thank Bronwyn Poole, Greg Carlisle, Caroline Chubb, and Matthew Levin for their special contributions of time and insight. Also Stacy Bruce, Rashaanda Cook, Ruth DeLeon, JoAnn Nelson, Kristin Pichaske, Jesse Purewal, Shekhar Purhoit, David Ransburg, Olga Rodriguez, Sasha Song, Michael Stepanek, Pam Tejes, Brian Tracy, John Treacy, and Marisa White—these Gen X and Yers have truly been my inspiration, my mentors and mentorees. And those who told their stories so others could learn: Geoff Bolan, Felipe Calderon, Blair Carnahan, Amy Halliburton, Brian Kreiter, Eric Mayeda, Michael McFarland, Keith Richman, and Kim Woods.

Thanks also for the tireless marketing efforts of Janet Dow, Teri Schram, and Lee Shoquist, who have beaten down doors promoting eLeadership concepts.

Of course, much appreciation to the many leaders with whom I have had the privilege and honor of working, collaborating, and learning, including Kate Abele, Graham Alexander, John Balkcom, Mark Blessington, Karen Boylston, Roger Brossy, Nancy Cole, Dave Cook, Todd Cook, John Coulter, Richard Day, Jimmy de Castro, Mark Dice, Richard Flury, Frank Gatti, Liz Hinds, Sandy House, Lin Knapp, Ken Lawson, David Lebow, Eric Marcus, Jerry Martin, Ray McGowen, Jude Rich, Carol Roberts, Sharon Robinson, Vyla Rollins, Deb Schmitt, Steve Strelsin, Harry Tempest, Paul Teta, and Oakleigh Thorne. Also those leaders who have shared their secrets: Lawrence Baxter, Bob Beck, Dennis Harris, Dick Keyser, Brad Keywell, Mark Levine, Scott Pitasky, Andy Rosenfield, Carl Russo, Mark Segal, Garrett Sheridan, Susan Silk, Bobby Soules, Mark Stavish, Kate Swann, Dave Tolmie, and Lisa White. And to the countless others I have talked to or interviewed in hallways and on airplanes—I thank you for your insights.

Special gratitude to my family, especially my father, Frank Annunzio, who served in the United States Congress for twenty-eight years. He not only taught me the importance of being respected and appreciated but also demonstrated by example how serving your people is the core of true leadership. And my children, Christopher and Angie Rose, who both already demonstrate the leadership of the future.

Thanks to my brother, Larry Hall, and my trusted adviser, George Hogenson, for showing me over and over again the strength and compassion true leadership must embody. And to my dear friends Barbara Jean Fitzgerald, Alexis Sarkisian, Sue Silk, and Renee Tracy for supporting me every step of the way.

And to Julie Liesse, who penned this book, for her inordinate ability to listen, challenge, and create. Thanks for finding my voice and allowing me to further my mission in words others could understand and benefit from.

I am indebted to my agent, Denise Marcil, for believing in me and my concepts and for pushing Julie and me to be the best we could be. And last but not least, thanks to Dominick Anfuso, my editor; Carolyn Reidy, president of Simon & Schuster; and Bill Shinker, my publisher, for delivering the message.

Contents

Introduction

You've got it all.

The great job. All the right perks. The beautiful house. Wonderful spouse, fun kids. Even the picture-perfect golden retriever.

You've made it.

You have run your company—or your division, or group—well. You made some hard choices during your career, but now the company is streamlined and profits are strong. Even if you're experiencing some bumps in the road, well, you've made it through tough times before. You are proud of your accomplishments.

But these days, more often than not, you wake up and look in the mirror and ask yourself: What's it all about? Is this *it?* You may have made a difference to the bottom line, but something is still missing.

Then you get a little nostalgic. You were in high school, or maybe college, in the sixties. And what a magical time it was, a time of real change and passion: the civil rights movement, the push for independent thought, Flower Power, San Francisco rock. A time for commitment, but also a time for revolution.

You were a true believer. You were going to make a difference in the world. You were going to make the world a better place for people to live.

But the sixties turned into the seventies and you went to graduate school and got a job in business. Then it was the eighties and all of a sudden you were smack dab in the middle class, having kids, buying that house. And then it was the nineties and even though you've helped in the community, sat on the symphony board, and coached your kid's soccer team, it's still not enough.

Now you may be a corporate leader, but it seems like the kids rule the world. Your son does his term papers on the computer while simultaneously exchanging emails, talking on the phone, and listening to Smash Mouth on CD. You may be reasonably proficient on a computer, but you are never going to live in the interactive high-tech world that your kids do.

That serves as a constant reminder that you and your company have to come to terms with the electronic revolution, both externally and internally. You read every day in the papers about some new dotcom company that is inventing a better way to market and distribute products. How long will it be before one of them finds a way to put *your* company on the run? You may have started some eBusiness initiatives here and there, but the big picture is still unclear. Where does your company fit in the eWorld? Are there new products, services, channels, or distribution methods you should be exploring? Might you have to cannibalize your current business to stay alive? Frankly, the thought makes your head swim.

In the meantime, you have kids at work clamoring for new things: flex time, telecommuting, T1 lines. It all sounds revolutionary, even smacks of anarchy, but you know that they are right, that you can do a better job of integrating the company's technologies with the way your staff works. But how do you transform your company's structure and culture without losing control? And when you have transformed the organization, will you still have a place in it? All the rules that have made you successful appear to be contraindicated in the future.

Down deep you know that if you don't face up to those tough questions, your company may not survive the eRevolution. And then, even if you jump to some upstart high-tech company, or retire with a comfortable pension, will you have made the difference that once upon a time was so important to you?

Here's the good news: If you long for the passion of the sixties, if you are tired of fighting merely to survive, if you are ready to make your difference in the world, if you are ready to meet the challenge of a lifetime, you have a real opportunity right in front of you. We call it *eLeadership*.

This book is designed primarily for those of you who lead traditional American businesses. My goal is to prove to you that the opportunity of a lifetime may be sitting right in front of you: the opportunity to transform your company into a player in the eRevolution while winning the hearts and minds of your workforce.

You may be enticed by the idea of a fresh start at a hot new dotcom company. You may have even been recruited for a job at one of them. And it's surely attractive. You can leave the problems behind you, leave all the baggage of an established American business—its hierarchy, bureaucracy, rules, culture, and, perhaps, its disenchanted or even nervous employees.

But is that the easy way out? Many of you, I know, really care about the companies you have grown up with. I think that down deep, you still want to make a difference in the world and improve people's lives. And I am convinced the best place to do that is right where you are now. As I found out in the early part of my career, business gives you the opportunity to influence a huge number of lives.

In addition, consider what is at stake if you and other leading business people abandon traditional companies. Think of the jobs, companies, and even entire industries that are in peril because no one was willing to step up and help those companies redefine themselves to compete in the new eWorld.

As the marketplace changes and competition increases, every company's strategy and implementation of that strategy will be affected. That's why this book is also for those of you who already have entered the eWorld—perhaps to take over a start-up business—and have found, perhaps to your surprise, that though well intentioned, many of these companies are poorly managed. They have to fight the tendency to unwittingly go back to the old ways of doing business, which of course are the only models we've ever had.

eLeadership is designed to do four things:

- *This book promises to leave a company poised to do business successfully in the electronic world, using a five-step model that I have developed over twenty-five years of consulting but have tailored to the electronic era.*
- *The model will help you effect real change at your company by bringing the rhetoric of change to the floor—by eliminating the gap between what is stated publicly and what is implicitly encouraged on a daily basis.*
- eLeadership *will help you create an environment that appeals to top talent of both the baby-boom and the younger X and Y generations, and then to close the gap between the generations so that they can work together effectively.*
- *Finally, I hope to inspire you to stay in corporate America's traditional businesses with the promise that you may end up a hero—saving jobs, resurrecting corporations, and improving lifestyles.*

Why do I think eLeadership is so vital right now?

There has never been a time in history that has witnessed so much change occurring so rapidly and affecting so many people. There has never been a time in history when the way we treat our people correlates so nicely to how well we run our companies. We live in an era where for the first time in history, that trite saying "Our employees are our most valuable assets" is actually a business imperative.

Business decisions have always been based on economics—the allocation of scarce resources. But the economy of the twenty-first century is centered on intangible resources: creativity, ideas, thinking. And those are *unlimited* resources. In the new eWorld, the winners will be those companies that create environments to keep the best talent and allow the free expression of ideas.

The other factor, in my view, that makes eLeadership so critical is that companies and entire industries are in peril. Many have been lulled by the boom economy of the nineties. But the world around us is changing faster than many of us ever dreamed. Soon, businesses we considered staples in our youth may become extinct or be totally reinvented, and whole new industries that we never could have imagined will become the norm. The social ramifications—positive, negative, in the middle—are still unclear.

At the same time, we live in a world where the financial models of success have been turned upside down. For the first time in business history we have companies with negative profits generating larger market capitalizations than traditional industry giants. Also for the first time we have to say we really don't know where things are headed and what the outcome of the current business developments will be.

The only thing that we do know is that if we keep the best and smartest people and we put them in a room together and trust their judgment, we have a better chance than the next guy.

So that is the goal of this book: to help you create an environment that will keep the best and smartest people on board.

I struggle with the same challenges every day. I am helping my company and my clients reinvent business models. I need to collaborate with Gen X and Y kids to be successful. And that's why I am writing this book: because I *am* the person in the book. I am the baby boomer who wanted to make a difference. I am the leader confronting profound changes in the business world today.

I started out in the mental health industry. My first job was in a community mental health center. I documented much waste of money, time, and resources. But I wrote letters and never got responses. I was young and had a bad case of "savioritis"—I really wanted to ride to the rescue of the industry—and got really disillusioned really fast.

Ultimately I decided that the place where I could make the biggest difference was in corporate America—because if you could influence the way people were treated in corporations, you could have the most impact on the most people. It wasn't totally altruistic—it has allowed me to make a good living and improve my life, too. But I do think that I have been able to affect people's lives. I now feel that at my level, with direct contact with CEOs, I can have even more impact.

In the past twenty-five years, I have learned a lot through trial and error, through mistakes, and through not knowing what to do, about how you engage a workforce, how you can create an environment where talent thrives, how you can collaborate and spur creativity through a corporation. I have learned how you can treat people so they feel respected and dignified. I believe I have methodologies that can help you lead your companies into the twenty-first century.

Now, at a pivotal point in my career, I believe the world really needs the skills I espouse. How lucky I am. I want to write this book because I feel the knowledge I have can actually do good. Doing the ethical thing and doing the financially responsible thing are now both the same, and never in history has that been truer.

We could afford bad management in the past; we could afford the lack of leadership in the past. There wasn't the same level of competition; decisions weren't that complex. Things were not moving at hyperspeed. You could get away with it and still make money. But you cannot do it any more. People are too cynical, too discouraged. Everything moves faster, the stakes are higher, the questions are more difficult.

I hope that my experience and ideas can help you and your company deal with the challenges of the twenty-first century. I have worked with many leaders throughout many industries who represent enormous bandwidth in brainpower, integrity, and commitment—commitment to employees, commitment to delivering high-quality work, commitment to making a difference. These leaders have the ability to ask the tough questions and confront the unspeakable truths—and in doing so, have begun changing the future direction of their companies.

These themes have recurred in conversations with dozens of leaders in meetings, telephone interviews, and focus groups, on airplane trips and in hallways. We have tried to take the best examples from our research—stories from companies big and small, high-tech and low-tech, new and old—that emulate the patterns we've seen.

Although you'll hear talk about best practices from leaders of some hot, big-name companies like America Online, Amazon.com, Cisco Systems, and 3Com, we know there are dozens of books out there telling their stories. Instead, we have tried to focus on unsung heroes in business today.

These men and women are just like you. They are leading companies struggling to find their place in the new economy. They run entrepreneurial or midsize companies trying to grow and compete in a high-tech world—or they are trying to figure out what parts of their older companies to keep and what parts to leave behind. Their companies and their businesses are not necessarily the most glamorous. They are not necessarily focused on developing a comprehensive eBusiness strategy. But in one way or another they all are changing their go-to-market strategies and trying to rally the workforce in times of change—to create an environment that will not only survive but thrive in the high-tech world.

Our heroes are people you might not have read about. These eLeaders aren't Jack Welch or John Chambers, but leaders like you. They haven't been on the cover of magazines, but they are doing the right things for their businesses. They are demonstrating real leadership in tough times— rallying their workforces, increasing their market share, boosting their market cap.

Their stories will unfold through this book. You'll hear about AMFM's Jimmy de Castro assessing his management team and making tough choices for the future. You'll watch Oakleigh Thorne speaking the unspeakable truth about the future of a company his family had run for five generations. You'll hear Sharon Robinson tell the story about making a loud statement to facilitate real change at a beloved company.

These stories are about a different "e"—the environment. This book is designed to help you leave behind your old corporate culture and build the flexible workplace environment you need to recruit and retain the best and the brightest. The environment that is mandatory to be competitive in this high-tech world. The environment where new ideas thrive, brainpower is appreciated and rewarded, ways of doing business are challenged and redefined.

If you get it right and produce this environment, you will be able to build your business platform, gain a competitive advantage, and possibly be the first to figure out how to make technology really work for you.

1

The eLeadership Challenge

WHAT IF ONE MORNING you arrived at your corporate offices and no one was there?

Your marketing staffers had decided to base themselves at various client headquarters.

The salespeople, equipped with Palm Pilots, Thinkpads, and digital wireless phones, were operating in mobile virtual offices.

Because of economics, customer service had been moved to another city, as had your distribution warehouse.

The R&D team you assembled was a collection of brilliant thinkers located around the world who worked with each other on networked computers and the occasional videoconference.

Your support staff—accounting, communications, corporate counsel—preferred to telecommute, plugging into the network from home offices and talking to each other via email and fax.

Even your personal assistant actually was located at the offices of your corporate parent, five hundred miles away; you and he communicated via calendar software, pager, and overnight mail.

What if, sitting alone at a big desk, you realized you didn't need a corporate office building at all? What would you do?

Welcome to the world of eLeadership, where business strategies are fluid, workers are smarter and more demanding than ever, and the old rules of business just don't apply.

It's a world of global markets, ad hoc teams, telecommuters, email, videoconferences, online ordering, virtual offices, intranets, networked alliances, and instant information. And it's full of both challenges and opportunities for eLeaders.

What Is eLeadership?

eLeadership is a new style of business management designed specifically to guide top executives as they retool their businesses to compete in the eWorld.

In this brave new world, what does eLeadership entail?

eLeadership means shaking up your corporate culture and fostering an attitude of speed and flexibility in order to facilitate the internal transformation to an environment for the new economy.

eLeadership means managing the clash between baby boomers and the new, brash Generation X and Y workers—and finding a way to combine the talents of both groups to achieve success.

INDUSTRIAL AGE	KNOWLEDGE AGE
An office	A workspace
Quiet	Noisy
Single task	Multitask
Focused	Directed
Lifetime employment	Lifetime learning
Wages	Ownership
Unions	Teams
Culture	Environment
Accuracy	70% solutions
Play on weekends	Play at work
Seniority	Performance
Tangible products	Intangible products
9 to 5	24/7
Office buildings	Anywhere, anytime
Knowledge is power	Knowledge sharing
Competitors	Networked alliances

eLeadership means making the tough decisions that will set your company on the path to success in the new economy—and in the process save jobs, companies, and even entire industries.

eLeadership *demands* heroic behavior. It requires abandoning past business models and challenging current assumptions and beliefs. It entails breaking many of the rules we've played by for generations. It means sacrificing the comfort of the status quo in the quest for a new direction that will survive the eRevolution.

And most important, eLeadership ultimately is not about connecting technology, but about connecting people.

Says Dave Tolmie, CEO of yesmail.com, a permission email marketer, "The success of a new economy company is based on the collective capabilities of its people. Every company needs to be more collegial and less structured so that the collective talents have a way to manifest themselves."

Microsoft chairman Bill Gates echoed the significance of the work environment in his book *Business at the Speed of Thought:* "The most important 'speed' issue is often not technical but cultural. It's convincing everyone that the company's survival depends on everyone moving as fast as possible."

Reinforcing that comment, international eBusiness consultant Eric Marcus says technology represents only 5 percent of the transformation process. The other 95 percent of a company's metamorphosis is represented by the changes in organizational behavior and culture that are at the heart of eLeadership.

As a leader, it's not your job to worry about how your technology is set up. There are people more techno-savvy than you to make those decisions. Your job is more compelling, and ultimately, more critical: to create an environment where everyone can unleash their creativity. Technology is not an end in itself, but merely an enabler in the search for new products and services.

In the example above, eLeadership means challenging the accepted belief that running a successful business includes bringing the entire staff under one roof from nine to five every day. eLeadership may require trusting employees to work independently in scattered offices. It may force you to give up some of the symbols of the Industrial Age: hierarchical organizations, clear lines of authority—even office buildings.

eLeadership may force you to measure success differently, both corporately and personally. In the future, the world is going to measure success in terms of how many new ideas your company has generated and what kind of talent you're keeping and attracting. Meanwhile, you may need to reconsider golden parachutes, country-club memberships, and corner offices—things that were the measures of success in the past. In the world we grew up in, these were ways of saying, "I made it." But they have become increasingly irrelevant.

eLeadership may mean finding new ways to be a leader: new ways to motivate when you don't see every employee every day, new ways to communicate your vision and create a culture, and new ways to think about what a company is and what it should look like.

We live in a world of new technology. We are bombarded by it every day. The availability of new tools has affected every company; it's forced them to reevaluate their businesses and rethink their strategies on marketing, distribution, communications, and organizational structure. Even if the strategy ultimately is to have no eStrategy, every business leader has had to rethink his company's place in the world. The new world is about "ruthless execution," as Amir Hartman states it in his book *NetReady*.

Most of the stories in this book are not specifically about implementing eBusiness strategies, but instead are about strategy implementation: how companies like AMFM Inc., GATX Terminals, and DSM Desotech put in new business strategies to deal with increased competition and speed—and then how those companies worked to catapult new behavior. The same principles that guided these companies apply in today's world of ruthless execution.

There are stories about companies faced with the challenge and availability of new technologies—and how those company leaders handled it. You'll read about Educational Testing Service coming to grips with how new computer-based testing would affect its entire organization. You'll hear how CCH, a ninety-year-old book publisher, moved its products onto software and the Internet. You'll read about the trials of two large banking companies, Synovus and Wachovia Bank, as they created online banks.

Although the initial goal was to help established companies make the transition to the new economy, eLeadership is not just for the traditional company. It's really about the kinds of leadership practices needed in the world we live in. And sometimes, though start-ups and dotcoms have fast-paced environments and stock options for everyone, the leaders sound and look and taste much like the leaders of the past.

Having visited many start-ups, my experience is that there's a surprising amount of hierarchical behavior and old-line thinking in start-up companies. Once you get past the funky locations and pool tables, they can look just like any Industrial Age company, with employee cubicle size determined by rank. In fact, it's my impression that start-ups are finding themselves working hard to protect the cachet of the dotcom world—sometimes at the expense of their environment.

Oakleigh Thorne, who lead the re-creation of CCH, now is a venture capitalist involved with several startup companies. "What amazes me about these new companies is how they too have to change their culture," he says. "People can become ingrained in a culture in a week."

With that in mind, you'll read about the successes and challenges of big and small dotcom companies in establishing and maintaining environments that support new economy behavior.

So whether you are in traditional corporate America or at a startup firm, the rules of the new economy challenge you to be an eLeader.

You must have a vision for your company. You need to create an environment where ideas flourish and can be challenged. You need to deal with employees expediently and fairly. You need to communicate and inspire your workforce.

Creating an environment for the new economy is not just a matter of getting up and telling your workforce that you want and need new behavior. It has to be more than symbolic gestures.

"If you open up 'new' old companies, you'll see they look a lot like the 'old' old companies," says Carl Russo, the entrepreneur whose Cerent Corp. became part of Cisco Systems in 1999. "The dress code has changed, which is really neat. But I'm not sure that it has anything to do with the core value set the company uses day to day. I think it's hard to cut at the core of that."

That's your challenge. eLeadership requires creating a workplace where new behavior is encouraged. It demands a new, irreverent way of communicating with employees. You must make sure this behavior isn't merely talked about, but really happens. eLeadership forces you to take the rhetoric of change and put it on the floor.

The Call to Action

The opportunity for eLeadership exists at the juncture of several powerful forces:

- The business world's need for leaders to guide the transformation to the new economy
- The speed of the changes in the business climate
- The long-term economic peril many companies and industries face
- The increasing reliance on intellectual capital
- The movement of Generation X and Y into the workforce
- The talent crunch in a booming economy
- The personal motivation among current business leaders to leave a legacy and make a difference in the world

Technology is creating business challenges not seen since the early twentieth century.

Spurred by technology, we are experiencing a fundamental reshaping of businesses, markets, and competition that's just as dramatic as that wrought by the growth of the auto industry—but the changes are geometrically faster.

In a survey by Nextera, 97 percent of business leaders said the rate of change affecting their companies is higher than it was just two years ago. Three-fourths of the respondents said that rate of change had doubled in a decade.

Speed is the first requirement of any eBusiness transformation, and it affects every other decision. To keep up with how quickly the world is changing, businesses must move from a strategic planning mode to a more immediate sort of strategic thinking—where decisions are being made "real time."

While you are learning how to make decisions on the spot, you might as well realize that in this new eWorld, you also will be making many of those decisions with insufficient data. No more six-month research reports or consumer studies. No more lengthy analysis upon which you'll base a carefully examined decision. The need for speed means that you will be operating more than ever using your instinct and expertise. In many circumstances, making a decision—any decision—will be more important than making the right decision. And it will take collaboration—the finest minds in your company working together to make their cumulative best guess.

If it's any comfort, the inability to rely on research and

analysis to make decisions may be a moot point because in many of the situations you'll confront in your transformation to the new economy there simply are not established best practices to follow. As consultant Eric Marcus says, it's not about best practices but *next* practices. You don't need to worry about consulting precedents or historical examples. There are none.

"A lot of success in this world comes down to leadership and execution—and being able to sustain some sort of business model through a world of insane competition," says venture capitalist/eLeader Oakleigh Thorne.

Consultants who specialize in helping "traditional" companies make the transformation to the new economy say emphatically that successful transformations depend on three variables: how quickly a company learns to do business in new ways, how well it leverages the unique characteristics of electronic markets, and how well it adapts operational processes, management decision-making, and the organizational structure to the eBusiness world.

All three things, but particularly the last one, fall into the arena of eLeadership. Massive organizational change is on the way.

As we're moving at light speed, we must be willing to ask ourselves tough questions about the future of our companies. Which of our current operating assumptions need to be challenged? What new business models need to be explored? And, consequently, what new offerings, services, sales models may exist? What must we as leaders do to better serve the marketplace, our clients, and our employees?

And then, we must ask the questions that are the heart of

this book: How can we continue to retain and recruit the best and the brightest when competing against the magnetic draw of the dotcom world? How can we leverage our employee brainpower to assist us in answering these and other questions we face as change rapidly descends? How do we encourage the employee behavior needed to implement these strategies in a time- and cost-effective way?

An eLeader needs to maintain core competencies and address the future simultaneously—as he reinvents his corporate environment. If he does not, his company's survival may be at stake.

Focusing on People

At the same time that technology is changing all the rules about competition, market strategies, and organizational design, we also must confront profound changes in the workforce—and the role of people in making or breaking the transition to the new economy.

The move from an economy based on manufacturing tangible products to one of intangible products and services, where information is the new currency, changes everything about how businesses are run and particularly how employees are treated—because now your most valuable asset is likely the information in your employees' heads.

"In our world today, financial capital is abundant. Financial capital is no longer the problem. Human capital is the problem," says Andy Rosenfield, chairman-CEO of UNext.com.

But the corporate rules that governed American business for most of the past century are dinosaurs that frequently get in the way of establishing new economy environments.

Lawrence Baxter has one foot on either side of the fence, as executive vice-president in charge of Wachovia Bank's new online banking venture. Says Baxter, "Four or five years ago in financial services, the common talk was that the old-line companies were hampered in moving to the eWorld by their legacy (computer) systems. Well, what became evident to me was that the real barrier was legacy cultures and legacy revenue streams and legacy business models.

"My time now is spent managing the people side of the equation; I need to provide leadership in that area rather than worry about whether the technology is working or not."

A frightening number of large companies still have to convince managers that people really are their most valuable assets. One member of the senior leadership team for a global manufacturing company relates this tale: "When my CEO talked to me, he said, 'I know in my heart that people are the most important asset, but I think right now the rest of our management team doesn't really believe that.' He was really referring to the years where we ran the company as if machines were our assets and people were liabilities."

Just like this company, many corporations asked employees to check their brains at the door each workday. Companies sought team players with blind allegiance who would follow the rules. It's still a problem at many of our biggest and oldest corporations. One executive for a Fortune 100 company puts it this way: "The skills you need to lead a big, established organization today are not the ones you need to get you to the top."

In an economy based largely on intangibles, the competitive edge is imagination, and using your imagination to improve the design, service, packaging, presentation, and delivery of your product. As eLeader, your job is to ditch the staid old culture and create an environment that encourages and rewards creativity, imagination, collegiality, rule-breaking.

You need your staff to be creative. Increasingly, you are paying them not only to do, but to do AND think. You have to *trust* them to think.

"It's all about speed and how quickly people are getting out there with their product or their service or their information," says one thirty-year-old vice-president for one of our nation's largest financial services companies. "But with the traditional decision-making structure, that will never work. Because the VP needs to sign it, then the first VP needs to sign it, and the senior VP needs to sign it, and then that person's Executive Management Committee member needs to sign it and that doesn't work anymore. It doesn't ease anyone's work load or save time or money if it's still this long drawn-out approval or decision-making process. The company needs to trust that the employee will make the right decision."

Many younger workers already have given up on traditional American companies in favor of academia, start-ups, or dotcom ventures. Says one twentysomething: "The inner infrastructure of these companies is so strong that you can't break it. A few people with fire cannot break a history of non-activity. Why bother trying to propose something new, because it'll take you months to go through all these channels and there is no upside to it. How do you fight that? The barriers to actual real innovation in a lot of companies are very, very strong."

The Generation Gap

Many business leaders admit they don't really know what to do with these Generation X and Y workers.

Who are these younger staffers? They are our children: self-managed, independent thinkers (and former latchkey children). They are multidimensional multitaskers (following in our footsteps but with more technology at their disposal). They have a cynical exterior but deep inside crave passion and want to change the world. And they view technology as the enabler of change—not the answer itself.

Fundamentally, however, they are in a hurry. They can't wait for seniority and experience; they want to be judged on their knowledge and the results they have already produced. And that is where they clash with their elders.

Before you dismiss these younger workers out of hand, consider that we made them who they are. These are our children. For whatever reason, the baby-boom generation has been more child-centric and child-focused than any in history: interviewing for preschools; learning about child development; worrying about daycare, private lessons, and specialized camps; buying educational toys.

We have sat at the kitchen table and had conversations with them—something many of our parents just didn't do with us. In front of them, we have talked about world issues and questioned authority and challenged the status quo. We have paid to send them to the best schools, to cultivate their fine minds and expose them in turn to the finest minds. We have raised them to believe they have unlimited potential.

So we have given our children the promise of unlimited potential—then they come into corporate life and feel that they've been thrown for a loop because their potential is being hemmed in by the boundaries. They are told they don't know enough because they're too young. But they've been raised to have opinions, to think out of the box, to push the envelope.

Here's an example: One client's business was really starting to go downhill. One employee, a young analyst with an MBA, wrote a seething paper about what he saw going on there. Everything that he put in that memo was right on target. But his cocky manner stopped everyone. It made it difficult to see the content. We had done an assessment of this company's culture, and our professional findings were no different from what he had put in his memo. This is a future leader. This is a keeper. He needs some polishing but he's smart and cares.

And most important, young talent like this analyst really responds to a leader's passion about work. They want to believe in somebody who believes. They want to know it matters. They want to feel your beliefs. They want someone to see they're smart, pat them on the back, and someone who will give them an environment where they will flourish. They crave the support of an eLeader.

What Distinguishes eLeadership?

In the past, if you asked about the qualities and traits of successful business leaders, you would hear a familiar list: You need to be tough. You need to know everything about your business, industry, and company. You need to be able to know what to do in any given situation. You need to be able to wield power and delegate effectively. You need to be able to issue effective orders. You need to be able to maintain control. You need to manage the flow of information. "Knowledge is power," was the Industrial Age mantra.

Sounds a lot like George Patton.

Many business leaders in the past were like military commanders. They were directional leaders. They gave orders and told people what to do. They were brought up in an age that created great wealth using an assembly line mentality: "Stand up in front, tell the people exactly what needs to be done. And if someone does a really good job of following the directions, HE can be in charge someday."

But you cannot be that kind of leader any more. The Industrial Age ended twenty years ago. Today we need people's ideas. Innovation is a must. eLeadership is required to succeed.

After dozens of interviews and hearing scores of stories, I'm convinced eLeaders—those who are ready to take their companies and workforces into the new economy as well as those who already have succeeded—share a list of qualities that is quite different from the old command-and-control leaders of yesterday.

HONESTY: Honesty is the first distinguishing characteristic of good leaders today, because it affects the environment in so many ways. eLeaders share information as openly as possible to create an environment of trust. They admit when they don't know something—and frankly, with the volume of data available, no one person possibly could know everything. And they admit when—overtired, overworked, overwhelmed—they make mistakes. They say they're sorry and everyone moves on. Finally, they encourage and reward honesty in their workforce.

Honesty in action: Carl Russo says it was personally very important to him to create an egalitarian, supportive, collegial, and honest environment at Cerent Corp. "The litmus test for me was what happened when we made our first bad hire," he remembers. "It was like having an extra thumb; it just stuck out.

"About three days after the person started, the manager and I were chatting about something else and he said, 'I think we have a problem. I think we hired the wrong person.' We went through the issues and I said, 'If that's the case, what are you going to do from here?' The response was: 'We need to terminate him: Treat him fairly, but terminate him because it's not going to get any better.'

"I was thrilled. That was the absolutely correct answer. But having the gumption to step up right after making a hire and say 'I made a mistake' is something that wouldn't happen in most corporations. There you're subtly encouraged to throw dirt on top to hide the mistake."

RESPONSIVENESS: An eLeader needs to reflect his carefully constructed environment. He needs to be as flexible as it is. That means being available to listen to employees—and to act when necessary.

> *Responsiveness in action:* Harry Tempest tells this story when asked how he encourages the entrepreneurial spirit as chairman of ABN Amro North America: A thirty-two-year-old vice-president in the banking giant's technology group sent Tempest an email saying, "I want to show you something. It'll only take an hour of your time."
>
> To his credit, Tempest answered the email and told the man to come to his office, where he displayed a possible new way to access information from a Palm Pilot—a product he had developed on his own.
>
> "I said, 'Fantastic, let's go with it. Let's build it around and put it into a couple of products.'"

VIGILANCE: Even eLeaders who have succeeded in creating the new economy environment they need say that is not enough. Continued success means being vigilant in keeping everyone on their toes.

At America Online, the leadership team has weekly operations committee meetings to keep everything moving smoothly, and to make sure the environment encourages the right behavior. "We are an intellectual capital company," says senior vice-president Mark Stavish. "We need to give people creative freedom, make sure they feel connected to the business, and make decisions that are the best for the company—not politics. Speed is a direct function of how effective your leadership team is, and how effective their decision-making process is."

Dave Tolmie of yesmail.com says, "Over time people have a tendency to gravitate toward the mean. That's always a huge risk. One of the things I have to do is constantly reinforce that we're a place where we don't do business as usual."

Vigilance in action: Andy Rosenfield is chairman-CEO of UNext.com, an online educational resource. He's created a new economy spirit among his committed workforce. "You tell people, 'We're on a grand adventure. We are experimenting. We are financed by people who understand we're doing that. So be attentive to change. Be prepared to flex. Don't accept what we did last month unwaveringly. Be prepared to think it through again.' You'd think that would be good enough."

But Rosenfield says, "Even in an organization as young as this, you get these locked-in ideas. People think because they've visited an issue once and reached a consensus, that's it.

"I have to run around kicking people and saying, 'We have new knowledge. We have new data. Revisit it.' Or I write memos that even I think are borderline wacky. But I have to disturb the equilibrium."

WILLINGNESS TO LEARN—AND RELEARN: This is no longer a world of "father knows best." You don't have all the answers. You may have to learn new skills and acquire new information to stay on top. Part of an eLeader's wisdom is accepting that you may have to leave behind the tools that seemed so important in the past.

> *Learning in action:* Today Dave Tolmie is CEO of yesmail.com, but he grew up in the bricks-and-mortar—or the cereal-and-spoon—world of General Mills. When you ask whether his background has been helpful in his new economy career, he says, "There are things from my previous experience that are absolutely helpful. And there are things that you almost need to forget."

SENSE OF ADVENTURE: eLeaders share an ability to live in the world of speed and enjoy it. They are making decisions fast, with little information; they have to know how to draw the fine line between quality and execution. They have to want to be part of the moment.

It is like riding a rollercoaster—having a pit in your stomach, being scared to death but knowing if you just hang on you'll get to the end. For an eLeader, the excitement of the ride wins out over the comfort of staying put.

> *Adventure in action:* Bob Beck, general manager–people for Scient Corp., the hot e-consulting firm, says, "Sometimes, it's been like, 'Where are we going to get our next income from? What's our revenue going to come from?'"
>
> Beck remembers one particular time when Scient was less than a year old and had to make a tough decision about a client's business.

"We had reached a point where we had to tell this client that we thought they were going down the wrong road. We debated with them until they finally said, 'That's what we want.' And it wasn't what we recommended.

"We then said though we'd hate to give up the revenue, we have to tell them thanks, we're walking.

"Later on we were proved right. But that was a tough decision.

"You have to find others as well who are risk takers, adventuresome."

VISION: Great leaders throughout history have had a clear vision of the future and have been able to share that with their followers. But never in business has having a visionary leader and working for a company with a mission been more meaningful to workers.

"You have to have a soul. The business has to be about something, because in a market where talent is scarce, people will choose to do something they find more rewarding," says Andy Rosenfield of UNext.com. "You can't compensate with pecuniary differences for the ineffable part of what matters.

"I don't think most business leaders treat the communication of the passion of the business as their most important task—when clearly is has to be." For Rosenfield, the mission is "the democratization of education."

For many eLeaders, the vision reflects their own personal motivation to change the world. At Amazon.com, the internal slogan is "Work hard, have fun, make history."

Vision in action: America Online's senior management team, led by Steve Case, has been together for five years and seen an amazing number of ups and downs. What holds them together and what keeps their workforce motivated is a keen sense of vision—which starts at the top, with founder Case. From the start he had a clear and concise vision of AOL: a new medium as central to people's lives as the telephone and television.

"In today's world, to be an employer of choice you have to realize that people have lots of choices, including who they work for, and you've got to build a work environment and a company that really gets at the essential notion of what people want to do," says senior vice-president Mark Stavish. "And what they want to do is to make a contribution. And work with people they like to work with. And they want to be in an organization they believe is going to make some significant difference in people's lives."

ALTRUISM: Call it whatever you want, but the best of today's eLeaders share a strong desire to make the world a better place.

Sometimes that means fostering an environment that people enjoy.

Brad Keywell came from traditional corporate America, as did many of his colleagues. He says, "I've said it a thousand times: We all came from jobs that sucked. So the challenge here at Starbelly is: Let's not suck. We all understand what it's like to not enjoy what we do or where we are. The workplace is a malleable object to be created by us together."

Sometimes that means finding a way to give back to the community.

At yesmail.com, Tolmie has started a program called "Say yes, do good." An internal website lists volunteer opportunities; employees are encouraged to take time from work on a regular basis to give back to the community.

Sometimes that means providing the world with a product or service that improves quality of life.

Altruism in action: Brian Kreiter, a Yale University graduate, was walking around New Haven, Connecticut, and was struck by the number of homeless people. He wondered to himself if there was a way to help those people by tapping the skills and interest of college kids.

What started as a casual conversation with local agencies has evolved into the National Student Partnership, a nonprofit organization that links volunteer students with needy individuals to help them get training, childcare, and jobs. NSP now has more than one thousand volunteers in fifteen cities and a staff based in Washington, D.C.

In the meantime, Kreiter, just twenty-two, has started his own venture capital fund and is CEO of one of the companies he's incubated. He's used his corporate contacts and savvy to get NSP funding from such companies as Goldman Sachs and the Fannie Mae Foundation.

"I always picture us as sort of Robin Hoods," Kreiter says. "I'm always thinking: How do we get this stuff back to the people who really need it?" Kreiter's long-term goal: "To eradicate the distinction between profit and not-for-profit enterprises."

The eLeader's Path

The road to eLeadership is not an easy one. And perhaps the biggest challenge is learning to be comfortable in this new, less structured, less formal environment—where you personally might not be comfortable at all.

But there comes a point in your life where you need to face the fact that the rules that made you successful don't work anymore.

This is not about money. It's about the ability to examine all your beliefs about what success looks like and the willingness to throw them away. That's a hard personal choice. It's also uncomfortable. You may live in chaos for some time.

You could ride the wave—for most businesses, including yours, there's probably enough time, and enough money left in the till, so you could get by with riding the wave. You don't have to address the mind-boggling notion of an eBusiness transformation and the cultural upheaval necessary to sustain it.

You did your best, after all; under your administration, it worked. The history books will remember you as the leader who generated 20 or 30 percent profit, reduced the waste, cut expenses. But deep down inside there's a little voice that says you're not really looking at the tough questions.

It's your choice. You must ask yourself: Am I just going to ride the wave and leave quietly, or am I going to make a mess before I go—and risk losing? Because once you've made the decision to try to leave a legacy, you also risk having it not work. You risk failure.

You have a choice. You can keep your big corner office and settle for what you've got. You can jump ship to one of the exciting new dotcom companies—many leaders disillusioned with corporate America are doing so. But you also can stay put at your "traditional" business and change the rules. In the process, you might change the world—or at least leave it a better place.

First, take a look at how you can improve the work environment through intergenerational cooperation—by bringing out the best of the boomers and the Gen X and Y talent.

Then five steps will take you on the path to eLeadership:

1. Win the revolution by accepting the fact that you can't win every battle: Take a hard look at your workforce and make fair but tough decisions.
2. Get brutally honest with yourself and your company. Ask the unaskable questions and speak the unspeakable truths.
3. Make loud statements about your commitment to change.
4. Communicate irreverently.
5. Create an environment that recognizes and rewards heroes—especially the unsung heroes, those breaking the rules of the past.

You want to be, in consultant Eric Marcus's words, the "digital alchemist" who turns a business that was created in the Industrial Age into a Digital Age success story. That may require launching a revolution. It may get messy.

A real revolution is all about:

- Breaking rules
- Busting models
- Asking the toughest questions
- Facing the unspeakable facts
- Breaking the code of silence
- Working against the odds
- Tackling problems
- Challenging assumptions

But consider the possible payoff. Ultimately, it's all about becoming and creating heroes. And if you launch a revolution, you may end up a hero.

TOUGH QUESTIONS FOR eLEADERS

The new economy culture requires turning old rules and systems upside down. I have been pushing CEOs for a long time to understand this concept and to begin thinking with an eLeader mind-set. Below are the types of questions every eLeader must ask himself as he begins challenging the established ways of doing business in search of something better. See if these questions get you thinking like an eLeader.

- *What if the rules that had made you successful were now the cause of your current problems?*
- *What if employees were smart and didn't need to be told what to do?*
- *What if you admitted your mistakes publicly?*
- *What if the name of the game was personal fulfillment rather than power and wealth?*
- *What if the biggest threat to your company's future was employee dissatisfaction?*
- *What if people did their best work at home?*
- *What if you gave everyone in the company a chance to make more money than the CEO?*
- *What if the CEO's office was smaller than those of his employees?*
- *What if your office building was destroyed by fire; would you rebuild it?*
- *What if everyone had access to information?*
- *What if the worst corporate sin was boredom?*
- *What if failure was defined as not taking chances?*
- *What if the winner in the race was the company that created the most jobs?*
- *What if the key to success was working with the competition?*
- *What if winning meant giving your product away?*
- *What if the only way to save your company was to destroy it?*

2

The Baby Boom Meets X & Y

THE FUTURE OF BUSINESS is a collaborative one—as never before in history.

Your business needs to work closely with those who distribute your products and those who manufacture your products (or those who have outsourced manufacturing to you). You must work with global partners, networked alliances, marketing partners, parent companies, sister divisions, regulatory bodies, and in many cases, competitors—as industries establish new distribution channels and technological standards.

But more than any other partnership, the future of your business rests, I firmly believe, on your ability to get distinct generations of individuals collaborating in the workplace.

Like many of you, I am a baby boomer. Many of my "kids" at work are members of Generation X. Just entering the workforce are the first of the baby boomlet—Generation Y.

I have heard the complaints from my fellow boomers: These kids are spoiled. They are pushy. They want everything this minute. They think they know everything—and they are only twenty-five years old!

Likewise, I've received feedback from the Xers, who gripe that their boomer bosses—or employees—are uptight sticks in the mud who never will give a new idea a fair shot.

How can these generations—each with very different work styles, personal goals, and expectations—collaborate so that everyone wins? How do we blend our knowledge, skills, and talents in a way that produces the best result for our companies?

For eLeaders, the first step is understanding who these emerging generations of workers and managers are.

Kevin's Story

In 1995, while waiting to graduate from Stanford University with a liberal arts degree and weighing law school, Kevin decided—for the heck of it—to take a couple of interviews with companies that were recruiting on campus.

Somewhat to his surprise, he accepted a job in the corporate planning department of a large media and entertainment company. Law school could wait; he thought the job experience would look good on his resume. "You get convinced that this is the sort of place where you can get a good education, learn a lot of stuff," Kevin says.

It didn't take long on the job for Kevin to realize "it wasn't what I wanted to be doing." He wasn't enthused about the financial end of business. And it wasn't the kind of place he wanted to spend his time.

"I just did not want to get up and do it every day," he says.

He found the environment of a big traditional American company "very bureaucratic and unempowering."

"I think people want to do something that makes them feel like they are making a difference," says Kevin. "And it's very clear, if you are an intelligent person at the very bottom level of a big company, that opportunity is fairly limited. And in a world where there are so many options, why would you want to work there—especially in this booming job market?"

After a year in that first job, Kevin found an opportunity in an entrepreneurial wing of the company. The pay was good and the company promised to leave this group of staffers largely alone. But after moving, he found things weren't really different at all.

Fortuitously, he got a call from a headhunter who offered a job with a twenty-person Internet startup company based in San Francisco. Kevin would have to take a 40 percent salary cut, but there were stock options. He didn't really think twice about leaving his big employer after less than a year and a half.

"I really did want to move to a place that I thought was more fun," he says. "It wasn't even the money, because the Internet wasn't even hot back then."

Once he got there, Kevin loved the start-up environment. "It was much younger, nobody really over thirtysomething. You could watch your visitor numbers and revenue increase every day. It was very exciting."

He was hooked. When the San Francisco company was acquired by one of the big Internet companies after only six months, he stayed on. But again, he was disenchanted. "It wasn't that much fun," he says. "When you are used to thirty people, the bureaucracy of even a five-hundred-person company is very encumbering."

Then while he was back thinking about graduate school, some friends approached him about a second start-up idea.

Eight friends founded an Internet company, sought financial help, and grew to about fifty staffers. Then déjà vu: Yet another big fish came in and swallowed them. Once again, Kevin had the opportunity to look around and find something that interested him at his new parent company. No sale.

Instead, Kevin and his start-up friends have now created a third venture—Kevin says it's "just another Internet company"—helped by $2 million in venture capital raised virtually overnight. Kevin manages business development at the new company. It's his seventh job in five years since college graduation.

At one point he'd been accepted by the business schools at Stanford and Harvard. But by that time, he says, "It just didn't make a heck of a lot of sense to go back to school."

Now twenty-six, Kevin says that if all goes reasonably well, he should be worth more than $20 million by the time he turns thirty. He has a big house in California with no real furniture, but two arcade games. He works twelve-hour days—sometimes more—and doesn't mind it "as long as it's fun."

So what will he be doing in ten or twenty years? Maybe he

will dedicate his work time to "community stuff," or do something in the entertainment market. But the one thing Kevin can't picture is going back to work for a big, traditional American company.

"It's very difficult for those big old-fashioned companies to retain people right now," he says. "There is just no motivation to stay. You are held down, you get paid less to do stuff that's not as fun, and to work in an environment where you don't have as much impact—for people who arguably aren't as interested in moving ahead as you."

And, he says, "A paycheck just has no leverage over me."

If you are an eLeader, this is your challenge. How do you make Generation Xers like Kevin—the best of the best—stay with you or come back to you? What can you do to understand them and work more effectively with them? How can you help create an environment they find interesting and where they will flourish?

The X Factor

First, let's look at who they are. There are approximately 44 million members of Generation X, born from the early 1960s through the late 1970s. They've been called the Baby Busters, and they are a significantly smaller group than the Baby Boom generation they follow.

The Xers are not all as smart and lucky as Kevin. But like him, they are confident, independent, and convinced that they are the key to their own success. After all, they know what it's like to be on their own: The U.S. divorce rate doubled between 1965 and 1977, as did the percentage of children born outside marriage. That means many Xers grew up in single-parent households, with working mothers and both more responsibility and more independence.

Their confidence in themselves and their future probably also reflects the fact that Xers have not lived through a large-scale war or prolonged economic downturn. Some call them "bull market babies."

Having much responsibility thrown at them at an earlier age has made them adept multitaskers. They do a lot of things at once, including working and playing. With the availability of laptop computers, cellular phones, flex time, and telecommuting, they don't draw the same distinction between work time and play time that their nine-to-five parents did.

Maybe it's that big divorce rate among their parents. Maybe they're just busy. Maybe they are just that serious about their careers. But whatever the motivation, they wait to get married. Statistics show that one-third to one-half of all Americans in their late twenties have never been married.

So on one hand, Generation Xers obviously have made work a high priority in their lives. But based on their attitude, they don't seem to take it as seriously as we boomers do. What do Generation Xers say they want from their life and their career?

The Wish List

From talking to, working with, and reading about this unique generation, here's what they say they want:

Impact: You are right. These kids *are* pushy and in a hurry. Like Kevin in our story above, they want to make a difference and make it now. And that's one big appeal of a smaller company.

One Wharton graduate said he signed on with Andersen Consulting in the early nineties with the intent of making partner. But he bailed out after four years. "They raised the bar and made it more and more impossible; the time to be promoted to the next level became longer and longer," he says. Now twenty-nine, he is with the Internet division of a large financial services company—a big fish in a small and fast-growing pond—and loves it.

Another Xer was recruited by and signed on with a worldwide consulting firm in December 1998, months before he was scheduled to receive his MBA. But as graduation approached, he began to feel he would end up being "just another cog in the machine." He called the large company, told them he didn't want to join them after all, repaid his signing bonus, and took a job with a tiny consulting firm in Chicago.

Mark Stavish, who as senior vice-president–human resources of America Online has hired and worked with more than his share of Gen Xers, says, "People want to do something important with their lives. And Generation Xers are simply less tolerant of situations in which that isn't present. Xers are less talk, therefore they'll leave quicker to find something better."

If they don't leave, impatient Xers will go undercover to find a way to have impact. When a twenty-nine-year-old acquaintance of mine took her second job, at a very large banking company, she says, "I was bored out of my skull within a day of being here. So I asked for more to do." She was assigned a project that no one wanted but she loved, which helped. But she also has had to carve out her own role, sometimes without anyone's help. "I figure that they hired me to think, and to do what's best for the organization," she says. "So a lot of times I sort of do what I want to do and then explain later."

But a young star like this shouldn't have to go underground to have impact. And because she is underground, her potential impact on the organization is diluted. Chapter 7 will discuss ways to enhance the impact of these workers.

Personal accountability and personal rewards: To keep them motivated, you will have to treat Generation Xers as individuals. They want to be recognized and rewarded for their own work—both their successes and their mistakes.

One twenty-nine-year-old describes her experience with her second employer, a medium-sized services firm where she was the first new hire at the corporate office in more than five years. She "challenged things," reworked systems, put in extra time and effort. And was rewarded with the standard 3 percent raise and same year-end bonus as everyone else. "That doesn't let you know your hard work is appreciated," says this Xer, who shortly after moved on to a better situation.

The personal touch is not just about money, though. One reason thirty-year-old Blair Carnahan loves his employer, Synovus, is that "they value me as an individual and care about what's going on in my life."

A great challenge: When Kim Woods graduated with a degree in journalism, she briefly considered a career in advertising—but ultimately opted for a job in a small company. "I wasn't willing to wait. I wanted to go and find something that offered more opportunity and more responsibility right off the bat," she says.

Contrary to the image of Xers as slackers—perpetuated perhaps because they like to dress casually, work their own schedule, and do more than one thing at once—these young people ache for a challenge. Work is not just about paying the bills; it's a primary means of self-fulfillment.

Scott Pitasky is director of strategic growth for Amazon.com, and since 1998 has helped the Internet retailer hire hundreds of new workers each month—including five thousand in his first twelve months on the job. If that sounds like a frenetic pace, it is. "But I love it. It's extraordinarily difficult, and it's extraordinary," says the thirty-seven-year-old. "This is an opportunity to write on a blank sheet of paper."

Don't worry about overwhelming them. It's your job as eLeader to give these talented young people a challenge that brings out their best.

Growth and learning: Part of that challenge is the opportunity to grow. If they don't get it, Gen Xers likely will opt to leave.

That's what happened to one Northwestern University graduate who got his MBA in 1999 and then went to work for a top consulting firm. He lasted there only four months. It wasn't the salary, which was great, or the people, who were top-notch. "I was ready to blossom and learn and grow, and the environment wouldn't support that," he says. "At some point it dawned on me that they were not going to give me a frontline assignment. I wasn't challenged, and wasn't learning a lot." He joined an Internet start-up firm created by one of his former business school classmates.

Today he says, "At business school I was soaking up information, gaining this great knowledge base. Then the rate of learning slowed down. Changing jobs was my way of speeding up that rate of learning again."

They're good soldiers; they'll do their share of grunt work. But they need and deserve more.

And if they are ready to fly, let them. I have a twenty-five-year-old Dartmouth graduate working for me—smart, ambitious, dedicated—whom I chose to head one of our firm's three big initiatives for the year.

Rather than let them leave, give your Gen X stars the opportunity to stretch their wings at your company.

A chance to work with great people: Part of the learning and growing comes from coworkers. Smart, talented, energetic people want to work with other great people.

"Keep the hiring bar high," recommends Pitasky of Amazon.com. "That's a constant theme, no matter who we talk to. Ultimately, it's the people who really make the difference in the environment.

"The more of the best people you have working for you, the more of the best people you'll continue to get."

Fun: Working with great people can also make the work experience fun for those coveted Generation X stars.

For most of their parents and grandparents, "fun" would never have entered the equation in making a decision to take or leave a job. But these young people place a premium on fun in the workplace—and every other aspect of their lives. And they are quite honest and vocal about it.

"It's a blast," says thirty-year-old Geoff Bolan of his work at iExplore, a Web-based adventure travel consultant. "You are going to spend a lot of time and energy at work—you should enjoy it." Bolan, who loves exploring and traveling the globe, turned down a lucrative opportunity with a worldwide services firm to spend his workday immersed in his passion for travel.

Xers like Bolan, who wears shorts and Teva sandals to his office in Chicago's West Loop, find a casual environment appealing. "I couldn't do the suit and tie thing," says another Xer, who is working for a midsize high-tech consulting company. "I'm not a big jeans guy, but I like the fact that things are casual here."

Whether they're at dotcom companies or traditional firms, for Gen Xers fun also means a balance between work and home. As hard as these Xers are working, they perceive a difference between their approach to work and the attitude of their elders.

Our MBA who left his first job, in consulting, after less than a year says even before he'd decided where to go next, "I had already decided I didn't want to make a career in consulting. I mean, you look at the VPs and their lifestyles—you would think it would slow down but it doesn't. They always are running around at a hundred miles per hour, year after year. I don't mind putting in long hours now, but I didn't want that; I wanted to be in a more stable environment, where you could have a family life, too."

Here's a story related by a colleague at another consulting firm:

One of his firm's bright young stars was recruited by a pre-

IPO Internet start-up firm with all the right credentials: funding, management, top-notch talent, good business plan, and a hot market to pursue. Lured by all this, plus ownership and a big salary increase, this young star left his big traditional firm.

What he found when he got to the start-up, though, was no support staff, no time to get up to speed on infrastructure basics (like how to use the computers), constantly escalating business goals, intense pressure to go faster—and a sacrifice of virtually all his free time to his eighteen-hour-a-day, seven-day-a-week job.

Actually, he never got to the seven-day-a-week part. After two days, he called his old company and asked for his old job back.

Passion for their work: Xers may want to have fun and act casually at their workplaces, but that should not be interpreted as a desire to take their work casually. As cynical as they can be toward everything else in their lives—authority figures, religion, government, the media—they want very deeply to believe in what they do with their lives. When they have passion for their work, the cynicism melts away.

How do you inspire that passion? By convincing these young people that their work has meaning.

The dotcoms have been undeniably successful at that. "When people feel like they make a difference and they like the people they work with, they put out extraordinary effort," says Mark Stavish of AOL. "Ultimately, no matter what age they are, people want to do something important with their lives.

"I think the cynicism of Generation X is probably a function of being in places where that doesn't happen—where their work has no apparent meaning. A lot of them are really intrigued by going to work with dotcom companies because they say to themselves, 'Gosh, I'll be right there, I'll be able to make that difference.'"

At UNext, Andy Rosenfield says his young workers are committed to the idea of changing the world through online education. "I think eBay is a perfectly sound business, but at the end of the day it's about intermediation of Pokemon cards," he says. "We tell people: If you care about achieving something and changing the world and making a difference, then this is a place where you can do that."

Every leader wants his people to feel as Scott Pitasky feels about working for Amazon.com, where the slogan is "Work hard, have fun, make history."

"I love the feeling when I meet somebody for the first time and I know they're going to ask me what I do," Pitasky says. "I get butterflies in my stomach, because I'm excited to tell them. That never happened at my other jobs. It just didn't.

"When I say, 'I work for Amazon.com,' it's a great feeling."

What Makes Them Tick

In addition to understanding what your Generation X and Y staffers want from life, you will deal more successfully with them if you understand their motivation.

The best of them are very driven—sometimes frighteningly so, compared to those baby boomers who spent much

THINK BEFORE YOU SPEAK

Five expressions guaranteed to stop the other generation in its tracks—and ways to rephrase that get better results.

IF YOU ARE A BABY BOOMER . . .
Don't say: *"It's impossible—that idea could never work."*
Instead, try this: *"That seems impossible to me. Help me understand how it could work."*

Don't say: *"We've done that before."*
Instead, try this: *"Here's what we have tried before. How is your concept different?"*

Don't say: *"If you only had more experience, you would understand why we can't do things that way."*
Instead, try this: *"That sounds like an innovative idea, but I see these obstacles in the way of implementation. Let's see if we can find ways to overcome them."*

Don't say: *"It doesn't look like you put any thought into that."*
Instead, try this: *"Help me understand the thinking behind your idea."*

Don't say: *"Let me tell you what you have to do."*
Instead, try this: *"We need to accomplish this goal within the following constraints. What are the possible ways we could do that?"*

> *IF YOU ARE A GEN XER . . .*
>
> **Don't say:** *"You're too set in your ways."*
> **Instead, try this:** *"What is it from your experience that makes you wary of my idea? Maybe together we can figure out what we need to do."*
>
> **Don't say:** *"You refuse to take a risk."*
> **Instead, try this:** *"You clearly see some danger that I am missing. Can you help me understand it and try to overcome it?"*
>
> **Don't say:** *"It has to be your way or no way."*
> **Instead, try this:** *"I would really like a chance to explain my rationale. I believe that if you understand the thinking behind my idea, the benefits will become clearer."*
>
> **Don't say:** *"You don't really want my input."*
> **Instead, try this:** *"This seems like a really good concept to me, but for some reason it isn't flying with you. Can you help me understand why?"*
>
> **Don't say:** *"Why are we still doing it this way?"*
> **Instead, try this:** *"Here's how we have handled this situation before. However, here are the problems I see happening if we try this approach again."*

of their high-school and college years "finding" themselves. "I'm sometimes shocked and appalled at how driven these young people are," says Roger Brossy, who at forty is president of my firm Sibson & Company, one of Nextera's legacy companies. "They seem to have known since they were teens what they wanted to do. Me, I really fumbled into what I'm doing."

They are less bound by rules: We grew up in a work culture where the bosses wore white collars, worked longer hours, and claimed bigger offices, and where seniority was honored. These young people are not as consumed with following standard operating procedure. They care about substance, not style. They don't care who is wearing the expensive suit. They don't care who has been with the company the longest.

They are more independent thinkers—and they will come up with innovations because they don't pause to think, "If I open up my mouth, I'll get fired." You'll get more honest, legitimate feedback from them. It's just that they may be harder to listen to, because they won't sugar-coat it for you.

On average, they are very confident and feel free to make their own decisions: Focused on our children like no culture before us, we taught them they had unlimited potential. They grew up with unconditional love. As a result, now they expect us to want them to be happy.

Growing up, my Gen Y son knew, no matter what he did— if he stayed out late, earned bad grades, or got in trouble at school—that the worst that would happen to him was that I'd be angry. He would always have a home, always have people who loved him. On the other hand, when I was growing up I believed that I had to do good things to earn my parents' love. When you have been raised with unconditional love, you feel much freer to be your own person.

They are less tolerant of bad situations: They don't like

politics. They don't have patience with bureaucracy. They get bored easily. They freely admit that they have no interest in following the career path their parents did, slowly climbing the corporate ladder.

Brian Kreiter, the twenty-two-year-old Yale graduate who opted to create his own companies rather than take a job in corporate America, explains his decision this way: "I think when you go to work for a consulting firm or an investment firm, until you reach a certain level, the institution has a way of telling you how and where your time will be spent. I guess I value my time too much. I didn't want to spend it analyzing the chicken market in western Pennsylvania."

And the truth is that they are living out our dreams. And as we've seen, if they don't like the situation, they will leave.

Our parents might have stuck out a bad situation for twenty-five years. We might have lasted five or ten years. These young people will be gone in less than a year. I envy that freedom.

They are generally not afraid to jump jobs or be fired: Again, going back to the confidence nurtured by a lifetime of unconditional love, getting fired doesn't have the same impact on a Gen Xer that it would have on me. They don't care how it looks on their resume that they jumped from job to job—or if they do care, they certainly don't care enough to stay in a bad situation. In fact, as one Xer says, "In today's work environment, it in some ways is almost looked down upon if you stick around. People start asking, 'Why'd you stick around for so long? Did you have no motivation to move up?'"

Although there are some signs that the cooling of the dot-com craze has left people more willing to stay put, the Bureau of Labor Statistics predicts that this year's twenty-two-year-old college graduate will average more than eight different employers before he or she reaches age thirty-two. That's a job change every fifteen months.

The head of human resources for a leading midwestern manufacturing company echoes that. "We have been able to attract great young workers," she says. "Our challenge is keeping them."

They are paying very close attention: As the eLeader, you have to be very aware that your actions are being watched. These young people are smart, and they are looking for what you do wrong, looking for any change of attitude or any inconsistencies between what you do and what you say. They are honest with you and expect you will be honest with them.

Recently, I really made a mistake and messed up a situation with one of my younger team members. What struck me was that he was so willing to let that screwup *be* the relationship instead of part of the relationship. I was not given the kind of grace I'd expect based on the history of consistent messages I have given him. I was barely given the benefit of the doubt.

These kids are so aware of the mixed messages they have been exposed to that if anything happens that makes them feel vulnerable, they rush to put on the tough, cynical mask. The saving grace, though, is that if you confess your mistake, they are ready to talk, to tell you honestly how they feel, to forgive—and to forget.

By comparison, I think members of our generation are

much less willing to talk honestly and to let bygones be bygones.

They are skeptical of traditional reward systems: They have grown up aware that the richest people are not necessarily the best, or hardest-working. They want money but it is not their primary motivator. They place little value on titles.

Instead of traditional tangible rewards, they seek intangible prizes. One person may long for a voice in decision-making. For another, the best reward may be flex time, or an arrangement that allows her to work at home part-time. A third may crave a particular assignment where he feels he really can have impact. As eLeader, you will need to be creative in finding ways to meaningfully reward them for their work, and in enticing them to stay with your company.

Brian Kreiter went without a paycheck for six months in pursuit of learning: He met a venture capitalist whose success he admired and asked if he could shadow the man for six months to learn how he did his job. (The two eventually created a venture capital firm together.)

They do want to be loved—and to love: These young people are hard on the outside, hopeful on the inside. It's not all their fault: They've been receiving mixed messages from us, and from the media. They want to believe that the television Cosby family exists, but they have developed a hard exterior—because they don't want to be disappointed. The good news for you is that although these young stars may have a different definition of loyalty, they want to and will be loyal in the right environment.

No More Labels

Because they are complicated, and because they think and act differently than we do, there is an unfortunate and destructive tendency to label Gen Xers and their behavior.

Which of these comments have you heard about your younger colleagues?

- They're spoiled.
- They want too much too soon.
- They're too negative.
- They're narcissistic/arrogant.
- They need too much attention/are high maintenance.
- They are never satisfied.
- They don't want to pay their dues.

Or it might be a situation like ABN AMRO VP Kim Woods repeatedly has found herself in, as an ambitious change agent within a big, traditional company. "I would say that some people look at me when I come up with new, different ideas and they think, 'Where in the world is she coming up with these things?' They look at me like I have two heads. I think that is a generational thing, frankly."

But the Xers aren't blameless in all this. I've heard the following labels stuck on boomer managers by their younger colleagues:

- They're stuck in their ways.
- They're afraid of risk.
- They want it their way or no way.

- They won't listen to me.
- They care more about what I'm wearing than how I'm thinking.
- They are too worried about rules.

Truth of the matter is that such superficial, unsympathetic labeling is counterproductive to your job as an eLeader. Whether you personally are a boomer or an Xer, as a leader you need *both* the wisdom and experience of the boomers and the enthusiasm, technological wizardry, and unfettered thinking of the younger generations to succeed in today's eWorld. Unfair, hurtful labeling only gets in the way of inter-generational collaboration.

You need to look at Gen Xer behavior through the looking glass and teach your managers to do the same—or teach your Gen X staffers to look anew at their baby boom colleagues.

And if you are a boomer eLeader, yes—the Gen Xers also need to look at you through the looking glass. They have to be fair with you. But they'll only do it if you pave the way by modeling the behavior first.

For example: You see a younger colleague as arrogant. But isn't he really entrepreneurial and independent?

You are frustrated that a younger worker is never satisfied. But isn't it that her standards are high and she's not willing to settle for less than the best?

You think your assistant VP needs too much feedback. But isn't that his way of saying that he really cares what you think, and wants to learn from you?

A twenty-nine-year-old colleague of mine tells the story about her former employer, a medium-sized consulting firm in the Midwest: "This company was so far in the dark ages, they could not see the light of day. It was frustrating: the systems, the mindset, the nine-to-five mentality. Many of the people I worked with would take long lunches and spend half the day on the phone. I was challenging things, looking for ways to improve things. But people thought because I was working before eight or after five, I was trying to get ahead or play games. They were threatened by that." My friend left the company after less than two years.

I was working with a client whose business was headed downhill. They had on staff a young guy, an MBA named Brad, who stood up at a meeting and told the executives what cultural barriers were holding them back. Everything that he said was right on target; we had done an assessment of this company's culture, and our professional findings were no different from what he expressed. But his tone made it difficult to hear the content.

Sometimes it's the boss who doesn't take time to figure out what's really going on. A very capable young friend of mine who works for an online wholesaler tried to handle a sensitive client situation on his own and emailed a status report to his boss. Before actually tracing the chain of events, the boss sent an email response lambasting the young man for sharing confidential information with the client, and doing it without supervision. Of course, if the boss had taken time to look at what really transpired, he would have realized that wasn't the case at all—that his assistant had handled the whole thing properly.

Here's my solution: You need to put emotion aside, honestly assess the situation, and figure out what a worker is trying to tell you when he challenges you like this. If you try to look at the situation from his point of view, you might see that this person is really trying to be helpful. Ultimately, young people like Brad really care about their companies. Rather than label him as arrogant or pushy, I'd say he was smart, passionate—and a keeper.

I think most companies' workforces can be divided three ways:

- The top 20%, who are the high performers, the leaders, and the agents of change.
- The middle 60%, who are the corporate equivalent of Richard Nixon's silent majority. They are loyal, they are good workers, but they are followers. Ideally, your top 20% is a strong influence on them.
- The bottom 20%, who are the chronically disgruntled— those who hang on to the past in the face of change, who actively fight new initiatives. You will read more about these people in the next chapter.

I would certainly place Brad into the top 20%. And companies keep younger workers like him around because they make results. But organizations typically do not create environments where many of these high performers are truly welcome. They certainly do not give these top workers the public recognition they should, as heroes within the organization.

Until that tendency is reversed, people like Brad will be outsiders within their own companies. Frequently, they will be forced to do their best and most important work under-cover, without the support and encouragement of top management. The potential impact of their passion and dedication on the "silent majority" of your workforce will be minimized. And ultimately, they will leave. After all, how long are you going to stay at a place where you are treated as an outsider?

In an era where talent is the most important corporate asset, your job as eLeader is to keep these valuable Gen X workers. They are the future of your company.

There also are pragmatic reasons for keeping turnover low. Nextera partner Jude Rich and his team have done extensive research linking high turnover to lower market capitalization. Why don't companies take the turnover problem seriously? "Companies sometimes don't know just how bad their turnover rate is," Rich says. "And they don't know how much it costs—in terms of the costs of recruiters, bonuses, and other goodies, as well as lost productivity. Companies become willing to accept industry standard turnover.

"But the result is that it cuts into earnings, and thereby cuts into their stock price and market capitalization."

Rich's perspective: "It's a tight job market, and it's already hard to get the right people in place. Why would you want to let them go?"

Your challenge is to bridge the generation gap and help your older workers understand and appreciate these high performers. You also must create an environment that keeps these young people with your traditional company, and keeps them doing their best for you.

Ten Ways to Make It Work

Let's face it: If you offer a job with a big, safe, established company with great benefits and a hint of lifetime employment to a Gen Xer, you may send him running to the next Internet startup. Some of your traditional strengths as an employer may now be seen as liabilities. Hard as it is to understand, the qualities that we boomers looked for in an employer—in the age when we all wanted to work for Procter & Gamble or IBM—frequently can be seen as negatives to young people today.

Instead, what you need to offer younger workers is an environment that suits their style, encourages their best performance, and lets them know they are welcome. It's your mission to show them that they don't have to go to a smaller company, an entrepreneurial firm, a dotcom, or a start-up firm to have fun and make a difference.

Here are ten ways to shift your work environment to keep your young stars on board and promote intergenerational success. Remember that while it's your job as leader to better understand them and to initiate new understanding, it's also your job to help your younger workers understand *their* role in intergenerational cooperation:

1. Challenge your assumptions: Don't automatically dismiss the Gen X approach. Try to find the logic flow in what they do, even if that means turning your logic upside down.

For instance: I facilitated a meeting among my younger colleagues recently. The subject was eBusiness ideas. Someone suggested streamlining corporate meetings onto the Web so that other companies could view and learn from these meetings. My instant response was: There is no way it would work. Of course, my paradigm is one of corporate confidentiality. But when I reversed my logic, I realized that these kids are from the *Survivor* generation, where the most intimate moments of life frequently are not just on display, but on display for millions to see. So rather than dismiss the idea out of hand, we are investigating whether there is a way to make it work.

Another example: I started graduate school at twenty-one and kept working and managing a household while I earned my master's degree—burning the candle at both ends. I never took time out for travel, or lengthy vacations. Now the young people I work with take time off at age twenty-seven or twenty-eight to travel the world, or to spend two or three years earning an MBA or another advanced degree. Then they expect to be reimbursed when they accept a job. The boomer response may be: "Gee, aren't they spoiled? Don't they have it easy?"

But think of it this way: These young people will get a better education, in business or in life. To them, the logic is: I want to be a really good student, I want to devote my time and energy to learning everything I can so that when I go out into the workforce, I'll be the best prepared I can possibly be. Or maybe it is just that they have learned how to enjoy life. I envy that approach and wish I had done more of that when I was younger. And as a leader, I have to ask myself: How can my company benefit from these vast experiences?

Bob Beck, general manager–people for Scient Corp., told me recently that he was hiring "twenty-seven-year-olds with twenty years of experience."

2. Let go of established norms: We must judge today's behavior by today's standards—not the standards of the past.

For instance, boomers have a different view of loyalty than do Gen Xers. Rather than complain about it, let go of your expectations and begin to evaluate your younger employees based on today's standards of loyalty.

To us, loyalty meant sticking around. To them, loyalty means telling the truth. I personally like their definition of loyalty better. If you stick around with your mouth closed, what good is that? I'm not afraid of losing those people who stick around just to collect a paycheck; I'm afraid of losing the people who care enough to challenge me every step of the way.

If you hire someone with the idea she'll be your employee forever, you have the wrong goal. If when she leaves—after three very productive years with your company—you feel you have lost, you are judging your company by old standards. The fact is, you have won—because you've done such a good job that people want your best staffers.

Carl Russo of Cisco Systems has a perfect way of expressing this need to accept new norms.

"You can look at it as: They are different and it's wrong. Or you can look at it as: They are different and it's wrong, but I know as leader of a company that I have to hire these guys, so I'd better find some way to attract them," says Carl. "Or you can just say: They are different, and it's wonderful.

"Get on with it. Get to know people for their idiosyncrasies—and love them for it."

Letting Xers be themselves—and loving them for it—

doesn't mean that *you* have to wear jeans to work, pierce your ears, choose an eleven-to-seven flex-time schedule, or leave for a new job in three years. But you need to accept that your techno whiz who may sport tattoos, a ponytail, or Skechers has as much value as he would in a crewcut, white shirt, and tie.

3. Create a free agent mentality: The employee value proposition has changed. When I take a job from you today, my responsibility is to get the results you have hired me for—at the moment. Your job is to give me whatever skills I don't have but need to do that job. And we both accept that those skills are marketable skills—you're not just giving them to me for this job, you are giving them to me knowing that I may take them and go somewhere else. The smartest companies are those that have accepted the new employee value proposition, laud it, and when someone is a success, celebrate it—even if he is a success outside the company.

Similarly, part of the new free agent mentality is making sure each employee is treated as an individual. Says one Gen Xer: "I always thought it would be interesting if everyone out there would be considered a contractor. And you're either billable or you're not billable. And if you're not billable then you have to leave the company. If you get pulled onto projects and you can bill your time somewhere, then you can stay on, you know what I mean? You set it up so that the true value of people is recognized and rewarded."

4. Create an entrepreneurial environment: Maybe you can't create the feel of a start-up firm at a company of ten thousand people with a long and distinguished heritage. But there is room inside your big, traditional company for pods of entrepreneurial activity. Why should your restless young hot-shots have to leave the nest to create something new?

With today's focus on eBusiness, many companies have done this by creating Internet businesses that have some degree of independence from the parent company. Witness Synovus, which has a team of a couple dozen people working on its new pointpath.com Internet bank. "We have been told to break out of the mold, go off on our own and build a bank— and not be constrained by internal hindrances," says thirty-year-old Blair Carnahan, director of business development.

But even the dotcoms face the challenge of keeping would-be entrepreneurs on board. "We constantly fight the 'I want to start up a company myself' syndrome," says Scott Pitasky of Amazon.com. "Our solution has been that we should be able to provide the best of both worlds. So on one end of the spectrum, we tell the entrepreneur who wants to start something himself, what better place to start it than in a place like this—where you have the resources and knowledge to not make the big mistakes that others have made. And at the same time, we have this amazing five-year-old e-commerce business for people who want to take something that has been built and then build it further."

5. *Establish structure, not rules:* Giving your employees structure means providing clear direction and goals, and explaining the constraints of time, budget, personnel, and equipment. Enforcing rules means establishing dress codes, approval processes, standard work hours, office space arrangements.

What you don't need is your staffers using their creativity

to compensate for your archaic Industrial Age rules. For instance, for one large distribution company we performed a cultural assessment—which involves observing what is being communicated by the building, office layout, design, colors, and so forth. During the assessment, I stopped at one person's cubicle because he had a very interesting poster hanging up. When I looked at it closely, I realized that the poster was actually twelve pieces of paper hung very close to one another to give the effect of one large poster image. I asked the employee why he had cut the poster into twelve pieces, and he cited a corporate rule prohibiting pictures larger than five inches by seven inches—the size of the smaller squares.

What that said to me was that this client was paying people to use their creativity to break the rules instead of using their creativity to push the company ahead.

The effective eLeader will give his teams structure—set the parameters very clearly and enunciate the goals and constraints. He will then let each team figure out how to get to that goal on its own—with a minimum of rules telling them what they can and cannot do along the way.

As AOL's Mark Stavish says, leaders should be "the keepers of the 'whats,' not the masters of the 'hows.'"

By the way, the team doesn't have to live with the constraints. Finding creative ways to get access to more money or people is not necessarily breaking the rules, and shouldn't be treated that way.

6. *Offer feedback:* There is no doubt about it: Generation Xers require more attention. They crave feedback. They are more focused on themselves, they are accustomed to talking things out. They want to know where they stand.

Unfortunately, many boomers find this annoying, time-consuming, or childish. Carol Roberts, vice-president–people development of International Paper, explains her company's experience this way. It's a very typical story:

"We have managers who were hired because of their ability to solve problems, because of their technical knowledge and their action orientation. So now all of a sudden these managers have a generation of workers that requires feedback, a lot of time, a lot of coaching. They're not equipped to do it, nor does it feel like fun. And they think to themselves: We didn't need it, so why do these new kids need that?

"What we basically tell them is: We can't make the time go away, but this is your job. We try to redefine the roles to say that is what you're supposed to do. Some get it, and some don't. Some do it well, and unfortunately some don't."

As eLeader, it's your job to stress to your senior managers the importance of meaningful feedback. If they don't "get it," tell them to think of how valuable such coaching would have been throughout their own careers.

But as eLeader, you also have to take responsibility for teaching these managers how to talk to their workers and give feedback (or hiring an outside resource)—to avoid any further communications problems.

7. *Give their work meaning:* Sibson president Roger Brossy, says his first priority when taking over his role was to define the company's purpose and communicate that to every employee. "I believe that the core of knowledge workers today wants to do work that has meaning. We have to declare the purpose of what we do; that gives people something to rally around. When the younger people in our firm are jazzed

and excited about something, it's because they have done something or participated in something with a client where something moved forward, something got better.

"It is our first and best defense against the talent drain."

Andy Rosenfield of UNext agrees: "This business has a purpose, and the purpose is to democratize education and change the lives of people all over the world. Because we have a purpose, I think we can recruit and retain people of excellence; they resonate to a goal like that."

8. *Bring them to the table:* As an eLeader, you know that the best of your younger workers are the future foundation of your company. It's not enough to just pay them more and keep them around because they get results.

They have something to teach you and your other workers. They have figured out what rules need to be broken. They know what's wrong with your company. Because they have something to offer your business, you need to make the rule breakers, the revolutionaries, part of your inner circle—your most trusted advisers. These young stars, who may have had to go underground to achieve their goals, will no longer feel like outsiders when they are embraced. And as you identify them, acknowledge their talents and success publicly, and bring them to the table, you and your company will move forward. As long as they are undercover, you're going to minimize their effort—you won't be able to keep them long-term—and you will minimize their impact on the rest of your workforce.

9. *Celebrate their success:* The smartest companies are those that do publicly celebrate the success of their emerging stars—and not only while they are doing good work for *your* company.

One of the companies I work with recently lost a senior contributor. What made this departure particularly notable was the way the CEO decided to handle it. He wrote in an internal memo: "Let's celebrate this. Let's make sure that we all take pride that one of our own is getting such a great situation for himself."

10. Take responsibility: I believe that most relationships are 50/50, but in leadership it's 60/40. That may not be fair, but I think it's right. Whether you are a boomer or a Gen Xer, if you are the leader the onus is on you to understand your workers.

I think you lead by example with the hope that as that person becomes a leader, they will assume a 60/40 responsibility—and that's how you get the payback.

As you take responsibility for making your relationship with your younger workers succeed, remember that people follow people. They have to believe you have passion—no matter what age they are. People want to believe that your company's mission matters to you, that it's something you believe in your heart and soul.

The Good News

As you think about the challenge of attracting and keeping the best younger workers, remember three pieces of good news:

First, not everyone wants to work for a dotcom. The volatility in the Nasdaq markets has made your old, traditional, established company more appealing to at least some people.

Nextera's Sibson president, Roger Brossy, tells this story: "I was most heartened recently to hear that one of our youngest, hottest-shot MBAs had taken a cab to the airport—and the cab driver was a man in his sixties who just two years before had been a CEO and founder of a venture-backed telecom company."

Second, the Y generation—the first of the 60 million just now entering the workforce—shows signs of being easier for corporations to deal with than the Xers. Researchers forecast that these young people as a group will still be very achievement-oriented, self-motivated, and accustomed to continual change, but also less angry than their Gen X counterparts and more motivated by money. Unlike the Xers, who grew up rolling their eyes at Woodstock and the Summer of Love, the Y generation also thinks that the sixties and seventies were cool!

Third, despite all that's been written and discussed about the clash of the generations, I see signs of growing respect between the baby boomers and the X and Y generations.

"The growth of technology's role in the workplace is simply forcing older managers who want to stay to change—and to respect the skills of the younger people they work with," says Kim Woods of ABN AMRO.

And even the dotcom leaders admit they need grownups to help them continue thriving, as they recruit top managerial talent from America's largest corporations.

Our start-up veteran Kevin, who opened this chapter, has

seen this happen firsthand. "When you bring a forty-year-old manager into a start-up environment, he seems to have a general level of respect for what the young people have built," he says. "And the young people are clearly bringing in the forty-year-old because they have respect for their ability to help grow the business. They're saying, 'I got us this far, but you can help get it to the next level.'

"That kind of respect pushes everything forward. Once everyone recognizes that, it's a beautiful thing. And the companies where that doesn't happen, there's failure."

Kevin understands that collaboration between the generations is key to eLeadership—because we need to use each other's skills and behavior to get further than we could on our own.

THROUGH THE LOOKING GLASS

Before you get angry or frustrated at intergenerational misunderstanding, try looking at it from the other person's point of view. Whether you are a boomer manager having trouble understanding your Gen X worker, or a Gen Xer puzzled by the behavior of a boomer colleague, you may be able to turn a miscommunication into a win-win situation.

IF YOU ARE A GEN XER, HERE'S WHAT YOU MIGHT CONFRONT:
When a boomer identifies roadblocks in a plan . . .
A Gen Xer sees . . . the boomer is set in his ways.

Instead, look at it as . . . the boomer is searching for keys to success.

When a boomer cites historical perspective . . .
A Gen Xer sees . . . the boomer won't try anything new.
Instead, look at it as . . . the boomer is identifying the foundation we can build upon.

When a boomer lists constraints . . .
A Gen Xer sees . . . the boomer lacks imagination.
Instead, look at it as . . . the boomer is listing the challenges we have to overcome.

When a boomer says one thing, does another . . .
A Gen Xer sees . . . the boomer is lying.
Instead, look at it as . . . the boomer is not perfect, and makes mistakes.

When a boomer puts on the brakes to slow things down . . .
A Gen Xer sees . . . the boomer wants to control us.
Instead, look at it as . . . the boomer may see some danger I'm unaware of.

IF YOU ARE A BOOMER, HERE'S WHAT YOU MIGHT CONFRONT:
When a Gen Xer challenges ideas . . .
A boomer sees . . . she's being too negative.
Instead, look at it as . . . she's trying to find new ways to succeed.

When a Gen Xer focuses on the future . . .
A boomer sees . . . she doesn't understand the world of today.
Instead, look at it as . . . she's trying to look at where the world is heading.

When a Gen Xer lists possibilities and options . . .
A boomer sees . . . she's too pie-in-the-sky.
Instead, look at it as . . . where could we stretch, what should we investigate?

When a Gen Xer challenges authority . . .
A boomer sees . . . she's not respecting my position and experience.
Instead, look at it as . . . she cares about the company; she may be a future leader.

When a Gen Xer pushes us to move fast . . .
A boomer sees . . . she needs instant gratification.
Instead, look at it as . . . she has been raised to believe she can do anything.

3

The 20/60/20 Rule

IF YOU ARE PREPARING YOUR COMPANY for the Digital Economy, chances are that you already are rebuilding your infrastructure. You are honing your strategies, putting in new performance and talent management systems, retraining your leadership team.

But if you really want all of that work to pay off, you have to be a leader whom people will trust, believe in, and follow. Your people—your source of intellectual capital—ultimately will make or break your success in the Digital Economy.

What are the leadership qualities you need to emulate so that you can create a working environment for the future and persuade your people to follow you? How can you close the gaps between your words and your actions and thus stop inconsistent messages that slow down your organization?

The answers are contained in a process we term eLeadership: preparing your organizational environment to make the

transition to the Digital Economy and to that new infrastructure, and demonstrating the necessary consistency in words
and actions during the change effort.

Frankly, I think helping your people cross the bridge to
the Digital Economy is the more difficult part of your job—
particularly if you are working at a company with an established, traditional business culture.

eLeadership is a five-step process designed to help you.
These five steps will show you how to attack your environmental problems, how to model and encourage the right behavior, and how to make your words and actions match—so
you can speed up your organization, inspire your young, cynical, or dispirited employees, and move forward into the Digital Economy.

The first step is taking a hard look at the people in your organization using my 20/60/20 rule, and making the tough decisions that will open the door to real change.

The prevailing wisdom in change efforts is that you must
convert your entire workforce. I think you win the war by accepting the fact that you will not win every battle—that you
will *never* convert everyone. In fact, if your goal is to convert
every last person and totally change your corporate culture,
you lose before you have begun the process.

But if your goal is to influence enough people to get your
organization moving, you have a very good chance of increasing your market capitalization, honing your competitive
advantage, speeding up your organization, and becoming
more flexible.

The secret is figuring out which people you need to influence. My 20/60/20 rule is based on identifying and using the

top 20% of your organization to both influence the middle 60% of the workforce and diminish the power of the bottom 20% of your company's talent.

AMFM's Story: Reprogramming for the Future

AMFM Inc. was facing a serious challenge. Industry deregulation had brought about massive consolidation, and AMFM had grown exponentially through acquisitions, to 450 radio stations in 1999. Instead of owning one or two stations in a market, companies like AMFM now owned five, six, seven—or eight, as it did in New York City. That change in the operating environment required a new corporate structure and style of management.

"AMFM was the quintessential entrepreneurial company," says Jimmy de Castro, the company's then-CEO, who set the entrepreneurial tone.

David Lebow, then executive vice-president, explains: "For years, we were totally focused on our top-line growth, new enterprises, and innovation. We certainly were not focused on the process of managing our company—or, frankly, on the bottom line."

In the old days of radio, AMFM had been extremely successful with this approach. And when it owned one station per market, it was extremely successful with station general managers who operated like "cowboys," Lebow says. "They would come in and start shooting and kill the other guys. And we needed that kind of cutthroat approach while we were building this organization."

But in 1999, AMFM wanted to make the transition to the new radio marketplace. With a merger with an even larger radio organization looming, the company also "wanted to have a surviving managerial entity," Lebow says.

Nextera's initial research showed AMFM employees loved the company and wanted to believe management could pull off a successful evolution—but everyone knew significant changes needed to occur.

After a thorough analysis, it became apparent to AMFM that in each market, its radio stations needed to be combined into a single business unit—to sell advertisers on radio marketing solutions as opposed to merely selling thirty-second spots. And with that change in approach, the cowboy management style no longer was appropriate.

AMFM created a new post called market executive vice-president, a manager who would oversee each market's radio stations. "The skill required to be a market executive vice-president is very different from the skill required to take down a competitive radio station," Lebow says. "The job became about bringing together groups of people who in the past had been fierce competitors. Each of these new managers had to a leader, to share a vision and lay out a plan for the future, and above all to build coalitions.

"Before you needed to be a marksman, not necessarily a leader."

AMFM worked with a research firm to analyze its management talent and compare their skill sets with the desired skill sets. That analysis helped the company identify its top managers: twenty people it felt would be not just the best market executive vice-presidents, but the leaders of the com-

pany's future. "They weren't necessarily the best radio sales-
men, or the best radio programmers, but they were the best
leaders with the right skills for the future of the company,"
Lebow says.

His analogy is a terrific one: "You have baseball players
who will hit fifty or sixty home runs a year, but will never
manage a baseball team. They are different skill sets." Just as
not everyone can be Magic Johnson on the court, not
everyone can be Phil Jackson on the bench. And vice versa:
Magic survived less than a season as Los Angeles Lakers
head coach, while Jackson was at best a mediocre player for
the New York Knicks.

AMFM was thrilled to put its new team in place. It gathered its new managers in Chicago for a kickoff meeting and
to model and encourage the new desired behavior. Those
managers then were sent back to their local markets to cascade the learnings throughout the organization—knowing
that they would have to assess their talent and deal with reorganizing their own management teams.

Corporately, AMFM still had to deal with the fact that its
senior management ranks were bloated. Now the company
needed only thirty general managers, instead of eighty, and
five regional managers, instead of eleven.

Frankly, some of those managers were not people who
wanted to be involved in the change process, Lebow says.
"They certainly weren't bad people, but they weren't change
agents." For others, as former CEO Jimmy de Castro says,
"The business had passed them by."

In addition, de Castro says, "There was a perception that
these senior people were being unfairly taken care of, un-

fairly compensated—all of those taboo things you don't want to talk about."

Making the right calls about key players was a tough time for Jimmy, who was personally close to many of those who needed to go.

"I realized that I could do the most good for everyone—both the employees and the managers I was letting go—to cut those managers loose and let them pursue their euphoria in life," he says. "They were in a position where they were not going to succeed. And on top of that, they were holding down the rest of the organization."

The good news was that those who were let go left rich, because of AMFM's successful merger. And today, Jimmy says, "I know I did the right thing, but it was the hardest management decision I've ever made."

For many good people, having to let friends go is an excruciating experience. They feel disloyal. But they need to redefine loyalty as thanking these people for their contributions, and then freeing them so that they can find something that makes them feel good and productive again.

AMFM had done its job: Top leaders had identified the behavioral traits necessary to drive the company's new strategy. They found a way to measure the company's top performers against those traits, in order to identify leaders for the future. Once those people had been identified, they were brought into the spotlight and made leaders of the "new" AMFM.

A meeting was held to gather the new leaders and give them the message of change and demonstrate the behaviors of the future. The newly anointed took that message back to the heart of the workforce—in AMFM's case, the employees of the company's 450 individual radio stations. Other communications devices and a revised pay plan reinforced the messages. The new leaders were clearly identified as the people in charge and the people to follow and emulate.

Finally, AMFM's senior leaders dealt with the people who were not ready to make the transition to the new world of radio—and dealt with them respectfully, kindly, and generously.

Today the company has merged with Clear Channel Communications, but many AMFM leaders—including David Lebow, who is executive vice-president of the company's western region—hold top positions at the merged entity.

It's a textbook example of applying my 20/60/20 rule.

20/60/20: From Top to Bottom

In addition to my consulting work, I am assistant adjunct professor of management at the University of Chicago Graduate School of Business. In that capacity, I have the opportunity and responsibility to stay on top of the prevailing wisdom on corporate change efforts.

Much of the change management literature, as well as the work of many consultants, gives the impression that you can totally change an organization. I don't buy that. What you *can* do is to speed up an organization. And the way you can speed up an organization is by targeting your moves.

First you must understand the following: 20% of your

people are your organization's high-potential high performers. But they don't necessarily hold the top jobs at your company.

They are the people who follow the rules when they can, but break them when they must. They are self-managed and inner-directed. They want to make money, but they don't work *for* money. They work for the thrill of getting the job done. Their passion is all about getting results.

They are ahead of the game—they have already been doing what you want the rest of your workforce to do.

And typically this top 20%, in conjunction with their teams, drives 80% of the work of your company.

The top 20% will stay at your company as long as the environment allows them to have the impact they want to have—as long as they are producing the results they crave and having a good time doing it. When the environment becomes so cumbersome that it's too difficult to get results, they leave.

These workers rarely leave strictly for money. But if they are dissatisfied with working conditions, money can lure them away.

On the other end of the spectrum are the bottom 20%: the miserables.

These are the people who believe in their hearts that the more they complain, the more they can bring back the old world. If they only complain loudly enough—if they convince you with the most passionate argument, whether it makes sense or not—they will somehow be able to turn back the clock.

In their irrational attachment to the past, they will use any tactics possible to put the brakes on your change effort. They will interrupt meetings. They will talk about you behind your back. They will flood the email system and the chat room of your intranet with complaints about changes and whining for the past. They will try to convince the rest of the workforce that you are making a mistake by trying to transform the company.

It is cruel and unethical to allow these people to continue hoping they can stop change. The world *is* changing. No matter how much they complain or how much they whine, the world will continue changing. New computer systems will arrive, the old dress code will be gone, new performance standards will be implemented.

But when you as a corporate leader tolerate the grumbling, you make three mistakes.

First, you waste financial resources. In most change efforts, 90% of the dollars are spent on the bottom 20% of the organization—in essence, trying to convert the unconvertible.

Second, if you continue to tolerate the bottom 20%, you feed their false belief that they can stop change.

Finally, you drain the energy of your leadership.

One research services firm clearly was in serious trouble; the company was experiencing record losses. Nextera's analysis described 40% of the workforce as "bottom 20." It was an extremely grouchy culture. The people were so set in their ways, they refused to let the world change. And predictably, this company's leadership spent a great deal of time fielding the complaints. It was such an exhausting and time-consuming process that these leaders found it difficult to do anything about changing and building for the future.

When your leadership spends so much time on the bottom

20%, they don't have time or energy for the people they really need to concentrate on—the "movable middle."

The majority of people in your workforce are outer-directed. They go to work every day looking for a pat on the back and some recognition that they did a good job. They are looking to be told what to do. They want a good paycheck at the end of the day. But they do want to believe in something.

These are the movable middle, the middle 60% of your workforce. They are the silent majority. And they should command a larger percentage of your time and effort during the change process.

As their leader, you have a choice: You can encourage the middle 60% to emulate your top 20%, or you can allow them to listen to your bottom 20%.

APPLYING THE 20/60/20 RULE

One of an eLeader's first tasks is identifying the top 20% of a company's workforce so that they can be publicly rewarded, privately nurtured, and inspired to help lead the change effort. At the same time, he must identify the middle 60% and the bottom 20% in order to send those groups the appropriate messages as well. Here is a checklist of typical characteristics of all three groups of employees.

TOP 20% PERFORMERS ARE THOSE WHO
- *Are self-motivated*
- *Are energized by challenging or complex situations*

- *Figure out how to get results in less time with fewer resources*
- *See a difficult situation as an opportunity, a puzzle to solve, or a challenge*
- *Are willing to speak honestly about the company's assets and problems*
- *Learn what they need to know in order to get the job done*
- *Do windows—or anything else in order to get the job done*
- *Encourage experimentation, and are always starting something new*
- *Mobilize teams to execute tasks*
- *Are comfortable making decisions with insufficient data*
- *Are not afraid to fail and learn from failure*
- *Know they will always be employable*
- *Execute real time*

THE MIDDLE 60% OF THE WORKFORCE ARE THE EMPLOYEES WHO

- *Are good, loyal workers and good corporate citizens*
- *Are outer-directed*
- *Need a pat on the back*
- *Follow, are uncomfortable leading*
- *Are reluctant to offer opinions publicly*
- *Avoid taking risks*
- *Crave recognition, and are motivated by plaques, rewards, having their photos in the newspaper, or their story on videotape*

- *Are torn between following the top 20% and listening to the bottom 20%*
- *Tend to play possum in difficult situations*
- *Avoid controversy*
- *Are afraid of losing their jobs*
- *Want to play by the rules*

BOTTOM 20% PERFORMERS ARE THOSE WHO

- *Question authority—but usually behind closed doors*
- *Complain about where the company is going and what the company is doing*
- *Discourage attempts at changing policies and procedures*
- *May seem lost when discussing changes*
- *Enjoy playing the victim*
- *Tend to react emotionally*
- *Are keepers of the past customs and procedures*
- *Enforce the company's implicit rules*
- *Are difficult to engage in constructive dialogue*
- *May sabotage communication and change efforts*

Nurturing Your Stars

To demonstrate to that movable middle what behavior will be rewarded, you must focus on your top 20%.

Those high performers should not have to break the rules to get the job done. They should not have to work undercover. They should be congratulated for their successes and be treated as heroes within the organization.

The top 20% does not necessarily *want* that recognition, but the middle 60% *needs* to hear it. By publicly praising your stars, be they individuals or teams, you let the workforce know whom they should follow and emulate. You let the cautious midlevel performers know that such behaviors will be rewarded, not criticized.

The first step is identifying the top 20%—as AMFM did. Create qualitative and quantitative criteria for top performers, or hire an independent firm to help you sort out your employees. (See list on page 84 for some qualitative guidelines you can use.)

Whatever mode of analysis you choose, here is one note of caution: Company leaders frequently will confuse the top 20% with the bottom 20%—as unlikely as that might seem. But both groups are challenging leadership. Both groups complain. Both groups are frustrated by the system and need to vent. It's just that their motives are entirely different. The top 20% is challenging you and complaining because they are dissatisfied, but also because they want to help fix the situation and move on. The bottom 20% complain because they want to maintain the status quo or go back to the comfortable way things used to be.

As an eLeader, it's your job to tell the difference.

If you are confused about whether a particular person is a member of the top 20% or the bottom 20%, engage the individual in a dialogue about her complaints. Sometimes that is the only way you can differentiate between the two groups.

First, let the person vent. Allow her to have feelings, and be empathetic. Give her time to calm down. Then say something like, "I understand you are frustrated; things are getting in the way of you doing your job. Let's talk about it and see what we can do."

If the person wants to engage in constructive dialogue, chances are she is a member of the top 20% of your organization. She is a person who moves past complaints to solutions. Her goal is to ready the organization for the future.

But if this kind of conversation doesn't satisfy her, you probably are dealing with a member of your bottom 20%. She continues complaining. Everything is wrong. There is nothing you can do to satisfy this person. Her ultimate goal is to undermine the future, and particularly the change effort.

I work with a top performer who can at times sound like a bottom 20%. This young person constantly is giving me a hard time, telling me what I'm doing wrong and regularly finding fault. He can appear arrogant and very demanding and rarely says anything positive.

When he comes to me with a problem, I let him vent. Then I offer possible solutions. And inevitably he backs off. He really is a member of the top 20% of our organization.

Once you have correctly identified your top performers, you need to begin cultivating their loyalty—immediately. You need to give them special treatment. You have to tell them that they are the future of your company—and that you want them to stick around.

You need to initiate individual conversations with your top 20%. These are the people who drive the majority of your company's work—the people who can make you successful.

In a world where there is a talent shortage, these people are more valuable than ever. You need to uncover what obstacles are preventing them from doing their best work. You need to figure out how to get them what *they* need to get the results *you* need.

If that is an uncomfortable exercise for some of your managers, try this: For the information technology department of one global professional services firm, we put the words on paper. We constructed actual conversations the managers could use to talk to their top employees, including things like:

> *"I value your contribution and want to know how you are doing during this change effort."*
>
> *"I want to learn about the kind of challenges/ variety/work content you need to increase your job satisfaction."*
>
> *"I will help you find career development opportunities because you are a top performer."*

After those initial conversations, each of your senior leadership team should follow through by "adopting" one or more of these high performers, to give them additional coaching or mentoring.

Protecting the Top 20%

You need to begin identifying and nurturing your top performers quickly, because the most dangerous situation a company faces is losing the top 20% of its workforce—either when they leave the company or when they lose their motivation.

That was the unfortunate case with one Fortune 50 company in the late nineties. This company was in peril. Its stock price was dropping dramatically, as was its industry ranking, because this company was not achieving its business goals.

As Nextera began its analysis, management maintained that the company had standard industry turnover rates—7 percent or 8 percent. They were worried about many performance measurements, but employee retention wasn't one of them.

A deeper analysis, however, uncovered the fact that most of the turnover was coming from the company's top performers. What should have been a top 20% was in reality only 10% of the workforce. That was a likely reason why they weren't achieving their performance goals.

Not only was the top 20% leaving, but the exodus was having a profound effect on the middle 60%. We discovered in focus groups that it wasn't the rate of attrition that worried the workforce—it was who was leaving. The middle 60% felt the company was being abandoned by its best and brightest—the people who got the job done, the leaders, the people who were really making the place worthwhile.

In a focus-group discussion about turnover, one man said, "If these great people are leaving, what does it say about me that I'm staying?" He had a pained look on his face. He was very troubled by the fact that he was sticking around.

When your middle 60% feels deserted by their leaders, and they are in conflict about whether they themselves should stay at the company—that's when they begin migrating to the bottom 20%. And that can have no good results.

When they are stuck in their emotional conflict, these overwhelmed employees tend to "play possum": They can't decide which way to go, so they do the bare minimum so that no one will notice them. You get their least effort.

You will not be able to speed up your company if 60% of your workforce is trying to get away with doing as little as possible so they won't be noticed. Not only are they slowing down your change effort, but you will begin to accrue the hidden costs of their ambivalence: increased absenteeism, increased workers' compensation and insurance claims, and decreased productivity and morale. Those things directly increase your cost of doing business.

Identifying and nurturing the top 20% of your company will help stop their movement out of your company.

The second way top performers "leave" your company is when they are worn down and transformed into members of the middle 60%.

At focus groups for a large professional services firm, Nextera encountered a man who was clearly a top performer at the company. He was bright, a group leader, a rulebreaker.

He said that when he had taken the job at this company, he came in with his eyes wide open. He knew he wanted to be different from everyone there. The company had a reputation in the recruiting community. He said the biggest problem in the company was that they didn't treat their employees well. Clients came first; management didn't show appreciation and respect for their employees, didn't ever stop to say thank you, and if they did, they didn't do it in a constructive way. Also, people were so busy that they didn't take the time to mentor or help develop talent. So this guy swore that when he joined the firm, he would be different.

Now, a year later, he said he had trouble looking himself in the mirror in the morning because he realized he was becoming "one of them." And he hated himself for that. The culture was so strong that he was getting sucked in.

This manager believed that to keep the best performers on his team, and get good financial results over the long term, he needed to treat his team members well. But in this organization, clients came first; client billings came second. There simply was no time to take care of people. And this manager was frustrated and giving up.

Identifying such dispirited top performers and immediately reassuring them about the corporate changes to come will shore up their support—and perhaps keep them in the fold.

In Chapter 7, you'll read more about how to deal with your top 20%, and how to create heroes within your organization.

Getting the Message Across

While you are taking care of your star performers, you also are sending out critical messages to your middle 60%. Every time you publicly praise someone whose behavior facilitates the corporate change effort, you make the effort that much easier. You are telling the middle 60% who is being rewarded and for what behavior. By identifying the heroes in your organization, you are letting the movable middle know whom to follow.

And in the fast-moving eWorld, you need as much of that middle 60% on your team as possible.

Look at it this way: In a typical company, the top 20% and their teams drive 80% of the work. Then there is that vast 60% middle. If you can get one-fourth of the middle—say 15% of the total workforce—to join and emulate the top 20%, then you have 35 to 40% of your employee base driving the work. And you will go faster. Even if you have a manageable goal, you'll be able to implement your strategy with less time and money because you have more people doing it.

But it may be difficult to win over the middle 60%. Many times, the middle 60% believes the top 20% are going to get fired.

Nextera was working with a global energy company on a cultural change effort. One of our first tasks was asking the company's "movable middle" to name top performers they worked with. Our goal was to create a videotape featuring those top employees and their success stories that would be sent around the company. After all, these were the people who were already modeling the desired behavior. We wanted to celebrate their successes—and perhaps inspire others to follow suit.

In focus group after focus group, no one would open his mouth. Even when we assured them that the CEO had asked us to do this, they refused to name names.

Finally, exasperated, we asked them, "Are you saying that your company doesn't have these people?" "Oh, no—we have these people," they replied. "Of course we do."

We followed up: "Well, then why won't you tell us their names?" They answered, "Because they will get fired."

At this company—like many others—the bureaucracy was so great that the only way you could get the job done was to go around the system. So the middle 60% saw those high performers as underground workers, bucking the system—and vulnerable to being caught and fired.

We never got names of people. Eventually some of the top leaders had to make personal calls to subordinates and assure them that the top performers they were naming would not be fired.

It took us three weeks to get enough names for a five-minute video.

Once you publicly praise and spotlight top performers, you will make them role models for your middle 60%.

In our sports celebrity–fixated world, there may be no greater worldwide star than Michael Jordan—whether he's playing basketball or not. Well, most people—particularly those in your middle 60%—want to "be like Mike": They want to be respected and admired for their accomplishments but also beloved as an effective team player. To really "be like Mike," those people need to know who the Michael Jordan in your organization is. Your job as eLeader is to tell them, "Guess what, those people you are afraid of, and are afraid will be fired—those are our stars. You may think that behavior is going to get you in trouble, but it is really going to get your picture in the newspaper, on videotape."

That's the way to move the middle.

Doing the Right Thing

While nurturing your top 20% and sending the right messages to your movable middle, you also must deal with your bottom 20%.

The easiest thing to do is to accept that the bottom 20% is dragging down your organization—and to deal with them professionally, humanely, and swiftly.

You should respect the accomplishments they had when they fit into the company. The best way to show that respect is to help them find employment at a place where they will be productive—because they are not productive at your place. They are miserable. And you aren't doing them or anyone else a favor by letting them believe that the old world is coming back.

Recently I had a conversation with the human resources director for a global manufacturing company that is going through a long and arduous change process. She divided her workforce into thirds, and said, "One-third of them are never going to get it." She then went on to say, "As the bar goes up and the expectations become clearer, I think they'll self-select out."

I told her that I disagree: There is very little likelihood that these people will leave on their own. Many of them will choose to rot in place. If you take your job as eLeader seriously, you must treat them with respect and provide them with a dignified way out of a bad situation.

That was what CCH did.

CCH was a medium-sized publishing company that had been successful for years with three long-standing product lines. So successful, in fact, that by the early 1990s the messy, inefficient organization had grown complacent and a bit arrogant.

The decision was made to change the management structure and corporate culture over a two-year period. Some people left on their own—"They couldn't stand what we were doing," then-president Oakleigh Thorne remembers— and others were offered early retirement packages.

But many of those who left were nearing retirement anyway. CCH's leadership knew it still needed to thin out and shape up the management ranks. So in 1995 they bit the bullet and created a program called "25 in '95."

The program was aimed at a group of younger managers, mostly in their late forties or early fifties. "They had come into the company in the 1960s and had never been empowered to do anything," Thorne says. "They had never learned how to build a business, or how to think about what they did in a business context. We had tried to nurse a lot of these people along into the new culture for a couple of years, and they just weren't making it." These managers were among the bottom 20% of CCH's workforce—and they represented the most expensive and influential part.

Thorne admits that CCH could have gone one by one through this group of managers and terminated each for performance reasons. But he knows that would have been a more painful process and that it almost certainly would have had a strong negative impact among the remaining staffers.

Instead, "25 in '95" offered full retirement benefits to anyone with twenty-five years of service with CCH. Basically, if you were, say, fifty years old and had been with CCH since 1970, you could retire early. Although it is much more common today, it was a bold move in 1995.

"We had an overwhelming response," Thorne says, remembering that about sixty managers took advantage of the program.

Overall, he says, "We reduced our cost tremendously, because these were people who were very capable of producing cost, but not terribly good at producing revenue. And they were administrators who couldn't make the change to our new culture.

"Their exit proved very beneficial to CCH as a whole; everyone who was left at the company and was part of the new culture felt very relieved. The feeling was, 'These people were slowing us down and now they're gone.'"

And surprisingly enough, there was a similar feeling of relief among many who left. "These people were being slowly tortured to death at the company," Thorne says. "They were unable to keep up with the new culture, and had grown very frustrated."

To help the survivors deal with their feelings, CCH tracked the activities of those who left in '95, and reported the results in the employee newsletter.

That had two powerful results. First, knowing that those who left landed on their feet helped the healing process among the remaining CCHers. But by publicly talking about the departed executives, CCH also sent an important message to its remaining employees: The leadership didn't feel embarrassed about what it had done. Many companies have similar buyouts, but because they don't believe it is the right thing to do, they act as the old Soviet empire did, essentially erasing those people from the history books.

As the CCH story shows, the most expedient and financially prudent way of dealing with the bottom 20% is to let them go. But many people aren't prepared to do that. If you want to keep them on, steel yourself and your leadership to disregard them.

Ignore them if you have to, but don't waste your time and energy on the bottom 20%. Ignoring the group as a whole will produce better results than catering to them. It's not unlike dealing with a toddler who's throwing a tantrum; every child behavior expert will tell you that paying attention to tantrums merely feeds the desire to throw more tantrums.

Moving the Middle

So you have identified your top 20% and identified ways they can thrive rather than hide. You have begun weeding out the troublesome bottom 20%, as quickly and compassionately as possible.

Now it is time to focus on the middle 60%, the heart of your workforce. They are the people who will ultimately make or break your transition into the New Economy.

If you are the leader of a traditional American business, you know that dotcoms and newer businesses have a leg up on you in terms of attracting and inspiring both the top 20% and the middle 60%. Companies from Cisco Systems to the

newest dotcoms routinely offer every employee stock options and the potential to become rich. Well-managed enterprises like AOL and Starbucks are terrific at convincing their
workers that they are involved in companies that will change
the world.

You might not have those tools at hand. But you can help
your company compete by taking a hard look at your work
environment.

What are the barriers in your company that inhibit
people's ability to get results? Do you know? Have you
asked?

There are several ways to acquire the grassroots feedback
you'll need to answer those questions:

- Focus groups
- Fax-back surveys, which employees can fill out and
  anonymously fax back
- Personal conversations with top performers: Assign
  each of your management team members the task
  of talking to five or ten high performers. Make sure
  everyone is asked the same questions.

Once you have identified the barriers to success, ask yourself: Do you have the guts to remove those barriers?

As eLeader, you need to identify and publicly confront the
cultural problems in your company. You need to personally
make moves to show the middle 60% that change is coming,
it is good, and they can be an important part of it. You need
to communicate with them regularly and consistently about

the change effort—and be prepared to manage the resistance that will invariably surface. And you need to celebrate your success stories, and identify your top performers, in order to inspire the rest of your workforce.

These are the next four steps of eLeadership, and they are all about motivating the middle 60%.

4

Ask the Unaskable,
Speak the Unspeakable

SUCCESS IN THE NEW ECONOMY depends on having an organization that is fast and flexible. To cultivate that speed and agility, you can effect institutional changes, hire and support the best of the younger generations, and hammer home the importance of moving fast in every communication.

But none of those efforts will be truly effective unless you also address the barriers that slow your organization. They are like speed bumps—stumbling blocks destined to trip up everyone in the organization. They are the implicit messages you send, the inappropriate behavior you condone, and the inefficient practices you support, usually without being aware of it.

As an eLeader, you need to help your organization identify and publicly confront these cultural problems in your company. You must encourage everyone, from your top managers on down to your line workers, to ask the formerly unaskable questions: Why do we do it this way? Why does management say one thing and do another? What are the unwritten rules of our company?

In response, you must insist that everyone in the company, including yourself and your leadership team, speak the unspeakable truths and be prepared for the cleansing nature of brutal honesty.

Companies are faltering because these conversations, which should be happening publicly, are occurring behind closed doors. Worse, the people talking about the company's most serious problems are those who have no authority to make decisions and change the course.

Or perhaps a company's top 20% is aware of the roadblocks and working behind the scenes to eradicate them. But the covert nature of their work conveys a sense of danger to the middle 60% of the workforce, who won't participate.

In either case, by not addressing barriers to success, the company is not moving as nimbly as possible and not meeting its competitive objectives.

Speak the unspeakable truths out loud, in unexpected places. The result is an invaluable step in gaining your employees' trust and proving to them that real change is on the way—while clearing the way for improved business performance.

One Company's Story

A Fortune 50 company was in serious trouble. It was trying to retain its historic organizational structure and beloved culture as industry conditions were shifting dramatically. But company leadership lacked a coherent strategy.

When the bottom fell out of the industry's pricing structure, this company—weighed down by its cost structure—began to underperform against the competition dramatically. Its industry ranking and stock price tumbled, it was not meeting its performance targets, and it feared it would no longer be able to attract and retain top talent.

The first step in getting back on track was uncovering why this great American company had stumbled after a long track record of success—determining the factors that were inhibiting progress.

It became clear early in the process that cultural problems ran so deep, there wouldn't be time to fix them—given the company's tenuous financial state. Instead, leadership needed an emergency solution: Copy the behaviors of the company's top 20%, those individuals who had found ways to circumvent the culture and get the job done. Leadership's mantra became: Go around the culture, remove the roadblocks, and break the rules if necessary.

A high-level leadership conference was designed to rally leadership to begin the push for change.

"Our leaders were running scared," said one company official. "They were trying to do things the way they thought upper management wanted them to work, rather than breaking any rules and trying new things."

In preparation for the meeting, employees from across the company were invited to focus groups and also sent a short written questionnaire, asking for both their honest comments on the issues facing the company and how leadership was handling them.

Employees faxed the questionnaires back to Nextera, to ensure anonymity and encourage complete honesty. "They were honest—brutally honest," said the company official. "Some of the answers were absolutely crushing."

FAX VERSUS FICTION

Your employees are the place to go to find out what is wrong with your company and what barriers will stand in the way of a successful transition to the New Economy. Consider these questions for a confidential fax-back survey or for focus groups designed to get the unspeakable truths out on the table.

- *What are the burning issues at our company?*
- *What are the "unspeakable" subjects that people talk about after meetings, in the halls, and behind closed doors?*
- *What are the concerns about senior leadership that are on everyone's mind, but never get addressed openly in meetings?*
- *What are people saying privately about our company's future?*
- *Are there rumors floating around the company?*
- *How do people feel about the changes being discussed?*
- *Are there unwritten rules that make it difficult for you to do your job?*

- *Why are people leaving the company?*
- *Do you believe our company does a good job of attracting and keeping the best and brightest?*
- *When you talk to colleagues about the company, what do you say that you would not say publicly in a meeting or to executives?*
- *What are the most frequently told lies at this company?*
- *Do you think people who tell the truth here—or say things that the boss does not want to hear—are rewarded?*

Employees answered the request for information with pages and pages of comments, concerns, and suggestions about how to fix the company. Wrote one: "I hope my comments help you improve the company I have dedicated twenty years to."

In general, when you ask for honesty, people tend to be more constructive than you think they'll be; in particular, this was a workforce that cared deeply about its company and its future. They were eager to get all this out in the open. They were desperate for answers and desperate for leadership.

When it became clear from the responses that the biggest underlying problem was a perceived lack of leadership, the meeting also became a forum for addressing that and other unspeakable truths that surfaced—comments that echo the unspeakables from other troubled companies:

- "We are not being led, just managed."
- "The leaders should be ashamed of their performance. . . . They are not up to it."

- "We desperately need a vision articulated so we can focus our energies."
- "They are virtually invisible. We rarely ever see top management."
- "We are organizationally structured for chaos, not accountability."
- "We are very good at processes, but we can't produce anything."
- "It seems that I am rewarded for *how* I do my job, not for what I achieve."
- "I am sick and tired of working under a siege mentality."
- "A culture of fear exists. We are afraid to call attention to problems."

The meeting needed to make a clear statement that things were going to be different, partly by addressing some of these taboo subjects out loud. It also needed to reassure everyone that top leadership was up to the challenge of turning around the company's fortunes. And it needed to energize leaders around the world—to make them personally responsible and accountable for the actions necessary to lead the change effort.

"As we got ready for the meeting, we applied the important rules," said the senior executive. "We prepared for something dramatic, sought to make people uncomfortable so that they knew real change was about to happen, and identified leaders who were accomplishing things—so we could celebrate their efforts."

When more than one hundred company leaders from all over the world gathered at the meeting, they first were confronted with a dark room. As the lights came up, they heard their top leader open the meeting by saying, "We are not on top anymore. And we have to figure out how to get where we want to be."

Tackling the perceived leadership crisis head on, the top leader—normally a sedate, unexcitable man—went on to give an amazing speech.

"I know there are people in this organization and in this room today who think I'm not a leader—that I'm not the right guy for this job," he said. "If that is what you believe, I'm here to tell you in the strongest possible terms: You are wrong. I *am* a leader . . . and don't underestimate me."

He added, "We don't have time to change the culture. We have to go around it."

The top leader then sat down with a respected local journalist who had been asked to moderate a question and answer session on the top ten unspeakable truths gleaned from the premeeting research. The journalist pushed the top leader to offer real answers—and make some on-the-spot guarantees to the audience.

The goal was to take on the unspeakables, clear up those that were merely misperceptions, and take action on those that were real problems.

For instance, attendees complained of a bureaucratic culture that took valuable time away from work to do endless reports for management. The rallying cry became: How do we eliminate unproductive work in order to focus on productive work? Singled out was one spreadsheet that had four hundred line items. "This is a culture that rewards people who fill out the four hundred items," said one attendee. Also mentioned was a process that required more than a dozen written reports. "If you cut out five, would you survive?" the journalist asked, challenging the top leader. "OK, then how about getting the total down to five?" The top leader promised to rectify the situation immediately.

During the next day and a half, the meeting proved an excellent vehicle for asking formerly unaskable questions, for speaking the unspeakable truths that were contributing to this company's dangerously bad performance, and for beginning the search for solutions to eliminate unproductive work.

One particularly poignant moment occurred when a midlevel manager got up and told the story of an important client meeting that had transpired recently. "We couldn't even get top leadership to come to our meeting," he said, naming names in front of the group as he expressed his disappointment.

To reinforce the value of speaking the truth, at the end of the meeting that manager was called up to the stage to receive a special award celebrating his courage and honesty.

The meeting was totally unlike any this company had witnessed. "It had people's heads in a whirl," said the company official.

To continue promoting honesty for the sake of positive change, the company took all the employee comments about the unspeakable subjects and put them on an internal database, where they could be seen by all. Within two weeks, a videotape with highlights of the meeting was sent to all offices so that everyone could vicariously share the experience.

Did the meeting help? In a post-meeting survey of attendees, more than 80 percent of respondents said they believed top leadership would make a sincere effort to change their behavior. Respondents rated the meeting 4.8 on a 5-point scale in terms of "exceeding my expectations."

Most important, within three months the initiatives begun at the meeting contributed millions of dollars to the company's bottom line.

Honestly, It's the Bottom Line

Getting your workforce to speak the unspeakables opens the door to change and can expedite improved business performance.

In the Fortune 50 company's case, airing its dirty laundry *set an improved tone for future communications* and a more honest relationship between leadership and workers. It began the process of removing the cultural barriers to achieving results.

The process of getting employees to speak what was really on their minds gave meeting planners *fodder for making the loud statements of change* that publicly kick off a big change effort. After all, what signals change more effectively than management's willingness to talk publicly about such taboo subjects as compensation, leadership, and company culture? (We'll talk more about other loud statements in the next chapter.)

This company was in serious trouble. But the process of speaking the unspeakable truths can benefit even strong companies that are on top of the world.

DSM Desotech was number one in its industry but worried about how to manage growth and further competition. Company leadership conducted a two-day meeting called "Beat the Competition." Attendees offered their ideas about what policies and procedures might stand in the way of the company's future success. Their lists then were examined by teams of workers. Task forces were established to address the real problems that emerged.

But as chairman Ken Lawson remembers, "It turned out that many of the concerns that were raised, when they were actually examined, weren't particular problems. They were opinions or assumptions people had made. And when people were able to talk these things through, those problems tended to go away."

As DSM Desotech found, speaking the behind-closed-doors assumptions out loud helped *get rid of imagined barriers to change* and set the stage to tackle its real problems. In the year following the meeting, the company posted its best year ever despite the downturn in the Asian economy. Speaking the unspeakables led the way.

There are several other reasons why getting problems out in the open can tangibly improve your bottom line.

Opening the lines of honest communication *opens the door to innovation and product improvement.*

Ken Lawson is an entrepreneur—always full of ideas. But he found that his DSM Desotech senior management team was reluctant to challenge his ideas. "They acted like a bunch of wimps," he says. "If I went to the staff and said, 'I have an idea,' they'd say, 'OK.'" Eventually, he had to confront the unspeakable truth: His managers felt they needed to do things "Ken's way." He had to tell them that he wanted them not just to implement his ideas, but to take those ideas and improve them.

"We respect each other more now," Ken says. "I have never been short on ideas, but frankly, better ideas are born when good ideas are challenged."

Getting everyone to communicate honestly *can help speed up your organization.* If you have all the information in hand before executing a plan, you should not have to do it over or repair it.

Finally, no matter how big or small the issue, *your employees are the best source for telling you what's wrong at the company—and helping you fix it.* But too often, they don't think you want to hear what they have to say.

When radio station operator AMFM needed to tighten up operations in the face of stiff new competition and a dramatically changed radio marketplace, it conducted a campaign to flush out the unspeakable truths. One of the taboo subjects that surfaced was a struggling division that happened to be the favorite project of then-CEO Jimmy de Castro.

"We all know it's the sacred cow," one employee said at a focus group meeting. Said another: "It was one of those initiatives that got jammed down our throats."

The way this division had been handled clearly was a source of aggravation as well as lost revenue. But as they vented their annoyance, it also became clear that the employees had solid ideas about how the division could be run more efficiently and cost-effectively—ideas that were never voiced, because no one thought they'd be used.

Yes, de Castro initially was disappointed and irked by the negative feedback. But after stating his feelings, he worked with his team to implement a better solution. No one wanted to get rid of the division. They merely wanted to improve the way it interacted with the rest of the company. And when some of the focus group ideas were applied, the division's performance improved dramatically. Everyone won.

Unlocking the Truth

AMFM's story demonstrates how a little prodding can unleash truths that help improve the bottom line. But the story also proves that if leaders do not make the effort to hear the unspeakables, these truths stay locked up and unavailable to help business performance.

Getting those solutions out in the open—encouraging everyone to do what is best for the business honestly and *without hesitation*—has never been more important than it is in the New Economy. To be competitive today, not only must you have a sound strategy, but you also must implement it well. With today's focus on speed, "the lag time between idea and implementation has to be zero," as Scott Pitasky of Amazon.com says.

Too often, your people know why you can't implement your strategy faster and more effectively—but they won't tell you.

Why won't they tell you the truth?

- They don't think you are going to listen.
- They don't think it's going to matter.
- They might get fired.

- They try—and you shut them up.
- And even when they are willing . . . it's tough.

At AMFM, for instance, Jimmy de Castro was a truly beloved leader. Focus groups showed, over and over again, fierce loyalty to Jimmy at all levels of the organization. For many employees Jimmy was *the* reason to work at AMFM.

That level of affection made it difficult for AMFM workers to tell de Castro that his pet division was a problem. It made it even more difficult for them to admit the company's most taboo subject: that Jimmy was a great leader but not a CEO.

Hearing that message in focus groups and written surveys was painful for Jimmy. But two good things happened. First, he realized that a great part of the problem was perception; when he shared information on all the CEO tasks he was doing behind the scenes, staffers' opinion changed. And second, recognizing some truth in the statement, de Castro turned over additional responsibilities to other leaders. And once again, everyone won.

Sometimes it's difficult for employees to be productively honest because the company has a history of punishing people who tell the truth.

That was the case at the Fortune 50 company. Stories circulated about the people who opened their mouths too often and were sent to a sort of "executive finishing school," where they were trained not to challenge corporate initiatives.

One manager who told senior leadership that the proposed reorganization strategy would not work—with documentation—found he was no longer being promoted.

Finally, one boss sympathetically admitted that he had been blackballed. The company never would fire him, because his group was tremendously profitable, but he'd never rise higher in the company.

Examples like these will prevent almost anyone from voicing an honest opinion. At virtually every company, there is some story that becomes folklore about how truth-tellers are treated. Ask your employees. They will tell you.

Employees may never know if that story is true or not, but it doesn't matter. They perpetuate the story to protect their own.

At one company, the tall tale was of an individual who had questioned the future of legacy computer systems. The story had it that this person had been banished from the information technology department and sent to a job where he'd never be promoted. People even told us the name of the worker. But when we researched it, the story wasn't true.

It echoes the frequently told myth about monkeys who want to get at a bunch of bananas at the top of a tall pole. Every time a monkey climbs up, it receives an electrical shock. Eventually, the monkeys who have been shocked will act to stop others from trying to climb the pole.

According to the story, that behavior becomes so ingrained that even after the electrical shock is turned off, no monkey will attempt to climb the pole.

It's your job as eLeader to convince your workforce that you really want and need their honest feedback—and they will be rewarded for their courage.

You must create one or more forums where employees can ask the unaskable questions and speak the unspeakable truths:

- Focus groups
- Confidential written surveys conducted by and faxed to a third party, to ensure anonymity
- Electronic forums: chat rooms, databases
- Individual interviews with selected employees
- Town hall meetings

No matter which of these mechanisms are used, you not only must allow people to speak openly and honestly, but you also must reward them loudly, publicly, and meaningfully for doing so. That may mean giving public recognition on a stage, with a prize or award, putting their photos in the company newspaper, or writing stories that trace the crooked line to success—by talking about the false steps as well as the right moves. But it also means taking your employees' feedback and putting it to use in your organization. That's the most meaningful reward you can give them.

The Big Event

The biggest, loudest, and most dramatic forum you can offer to speak the unspeakables is a kickoff event similar to the day-and-a-half affair produced by the Fortune 50 company.

These well-planned productions generally are used to initiate a broad-scale change effort, to inspire top management, or to confront a widespread problem, like the Fortune 50 company's leadership crisis. Although only one facet of the agenda, the unspeakables session generally opens the meeting—because it sets the appropriate tone of honesty and camaraderie, breaks down barriers, levels the playing field between leadership and workers, and tends to knock everyone off their feet, so to speak.

When Nextera helps plan one of these meetings, we generally use the information we've gathered through our fax-back surveys, focus groups, and the like to create a David Lettermanesque "top ten" list of unspeakable subjects. We share that list with meeting attendees right away, to get them thinking and pumped up.

Then we put the top executives up on a stage, in front of everyone, to address those unspeakable subjects.

It's usually smart to have someone other than the company's own top leaders moderate the ensuing discussion. For one thing, the moderator serves as a representative of the audience.

For instance, when a large media company staged its big change kickoff event, it hired professional moderator Susan Silk to run the session on the tough questions. Many of the questions revolved around the big issue of the company's impending merger. Silk cogently summarized the audience's feelings when she told management, "These people didn't come to this company just to have fun and make money. They came here for you. Now they are going through a sense of loss and fear. They are afraid."

A moderator also will increase the impact of top leaders' answers.

When asked these tough questions, the people in charge will answer as best as they can. But even the best of them are uncomfortable. They probably don't know that they are not answering the questions well. And the employees in the audience, even if they have asked the first tough question, usually have a hard time pressing for a better answer. It's their boss, after all, who's up there. And they assume that the boss dodged the question on purpose. So what would be the point of asking it again?

An independent moderator helps the audience by pushing for real answers. He helps the panel by giving them a second chance to answer—and they inevitably do better the second time. The executives didn't realize they weren't answering the question. They blush, they laugh, they stutter. They become more human and more likable. It's wonderful to watch these executives open up, and to gauge the audience response. It can be a magic moment for a company.

Management consultant Todd Cook was in charge of one of these big-event meetings. In preparation for the unspeakables session, he coached his executive team on how to answer tough questions. But because he didn't want their answers to be rehearsed, the coaching session didn't use the actual unspeakable truths.

The session was moderated by a prominent local TV journalist in front of some 450 company employees. The moderator asked the CEO one of the ten tough questions: When will a real leader step up to head this company? And as Cook tells it, "The CEO just got caught."

As the CEO began answering, the moderator interrupted, saying, "Wait a minute—this is management speak. Tell me what you're really thinking."

This happened again on the next question. Finally, the

CEO "got this huge grin on his face, turned to his fellow pan-
elists and said, 'Help!'" Cook remembers. "That moment
made him a hero."

The audience response exceeded all of Cook's expectations. "People couldn't believe this was happening," he says.

"It's not that these questions never get asked of senior executives. It's just that they come up with bogus answers that
don't mean anything. What made it so powerful is that we
pushed them for honesty—respectfully but irreverently."

That honesty can be one of the most powerful ways to motivate the top 20% and middle 60% of your workforce for
change.

At the two-and-a-half-hour global videoconference that
kicked off publishing company CCH's change effort, Chicago
journalist John Callaway moderated the unspeakables session.

"CCH asked me to serve as an advocate for those of you
who can't physically be here—and even for those of you who
are in the room," Callaway told the audience. "My role is to
push today's discussion for straight, clear answers to the
tough questions facing CCH."

Having studied up on the company and read the list of
unaskable questions, Callaway pulled no punches with the
three CCH leaders on the podium.

"You cut salaried employees' hourly wages," he began.
"You make them work longer days. You take away their
breaks. You shorten their lunchtime. You tell them to work
more. You cut sales commissions. All while you three were
enjoying hundreds of thousands of dollars of bonuses, and
while the stock is going down."

The audience cheered. The executives could only smile sheepishly.

It doesn't matter how they answered those charges. What mattered was simply the fact that the employees—through their representative—were able to pose the questions.

When polled after the CCH videoconference, 61 percent of employees said they felt more favorable toward the executive committee. That number was up seventeen points.

There was no doubt that the change effort was real and that the CCH leaders were modeling the behavior they sought from the workforce: They took risks, challenged ideas, and assumed responsibility.

THE UNSPEAKABLE SUBJECTS

Every company has its unspeakable subjects. But if you listed them, you'd be surprised at how the same forbidden subjects and themes exist in company after company. Here are some verbatim examples from fax-back surveys and focus groups at real companies.

- *Leadership does not do a good job of articulating our vision and mission.*
- *We have managers, not leaders.*
- *Our company is top heavy.*
- *Leadership is a "boys' club."*
- *Leadership gets paid too much while the company is struggling.*

- *There is no management accountability.*
- *Our best people are leaving, and our poor performers are not.*
- *Our compensation is not competitive.*
- *We are not paid for what we do as individuals; everyone gets the same rewards.*
- *No one cares how hard we work.*
- *Leadership does not do a good job communicating with employees.*
- *Leadership lies to us.*
- *Leadership is sending us mixed messages.*
- *Leadership tells us one thing but does something else.*
- *We talk all the time about teamwork, but there are too many silos.*
- *People care too much about impressing the bosses rather than doing what's right for the business.*
- *People are afraid of change/takeover/downsizing/merger.*

Motivating Constituencies

Speaking the unspeakables is powerful for your entire workforce. It helps your top 20%—the people who will lead your company and your change effort—uncover and get rid of the obstacles to change. It also allows them to stop working covertly and go public with the ways they already have been facilitating change.

As the covert behavior of the top 20% becomes sanctioned by leadership, the middle 60% of your workforce no longer needs to be afraid. You can spur them to partner with the top 20% in leading change.

Again, your goal is to convert one-fourth of that middle 60% to join your company's top performers. Then you will have a potent third of your workforce pulling together in the same boat.

Finally, addressing the unspeakables shuts down the bottom 20%. Your critics can have little to say if you walk onto a stage and address your company's problems honestly and publicly. Such a demonstration takes the wind out of their sails. They can't sit and smugly criticize you if you criticize yourself where appropriate.

In fact, as leaders publicly confront the tough questions, they tend to attract the sympathy of the workforce—sympathy that the bottom 20% has been trying to monopolize. And as top leaders become sympathetic figures, the bottom 20% is left looking like whiners, haranguers, and complainers. Their lack of interest in constructive problem-solving becomes clear.

You win on all three counts.

But there are two audiences for whom speaking the unspeakables can have particular importance.

First, creating an environment of such candor is especially appealing to your Generation X and Y employees—the ultimate skeptics. These are the people who are most consciously aware of the contradictions between your words and your behavior. They are astute observers of behavior. They pick up on every falsehood. But they also appreciate every push for honesty.

Second, it can be a critical exercise for your senior leadership team. As a small group, they have their own set of un-speakable truths that need to be aired. There are things about their group dynamics and the way they operate that may need to be discussed: who's friends with whom, what po-litical issues are lurking beneath the surface at every meet-ing. Just as getting the corporate unspeakables out in the open can free the broader group of employees to work better as a team, getting the unspeakables out within this small group of leaders can help them develop a better, more pro-ductive relationship. In fact, until these issues are resolved at the top, it will be difficult to resolve the bigger issues among the broader workforce.

When two large professional services firms merged, we staged team-building forums for the top leadership of the two firms. The frank, open discussions were so effective in promoting teamwork that when a dictate came down to cut costs by firing people, the team was able to work together to find the savings elsewhere.

At DSM Desotech, Ken Lawson had a problem getting employees to think beyond doing it "Ken's way." But nowhere was that tendency more deeply rooted than it was in his senior management group. And they found it ex-tremely difficult to break this dynamic.

Finally, one of the team members came up with this idea: If any one of the group was caught "just doing it Ken's way" and avoiding the truth, another group member was supposed to let him know he was "sucking up" to the boss—by literally making a wet sucking sound on the back of his hand.

This group of leaders was so accustomed to responding to Lawson in a certain way that they no longer were aware that they were doing so. But when one of them was caught and the rest of the group began making the suck-up sound, it broke the dynamic in a way that made everyone laugh.

Ken recently gave up day-to-day management of the company. Because his senior leadership group had established an honest working relationship, they were able to create a succession plan and make the transition to a new CEO with minimal disruption. They were able to have frank discussions about what needed to be done for the future of DSM Desotech.

The Hidden Costs of Secrecy

If you do not give your workforce a chance to speak honestly about their problems and concerns, that doesn't mean you'll shut down the water-cooler chatter. The absence of a forum to speak the unspeakables only means that people will be voicing these concerns out of earshot.

They still will speak the unspeakables—you can be assured of that. But they will talk behind closed doors, after the meeting is over, frequently with inaccurate information. These are the conversations people will have over and over again, instead of working. And you will have no opportunity to correct misunderstandings and misinformation. Misperceptions will be reinforced.

When the unspeakable truth is spoken behind closed doors, people use emotional logic to explain what you as company leader have not had a chance to explain to them. That means when they don't have the facts, people will reach a subjective conclusion to explain something that doesn't make sense to them. They make up an explanation. And human nature dictates that the likelihood of making up something *worse* than the truth is extremely high.

A large midwestern company had committed millions of dollars to a new total quality management system. Managers dutifully asked their workers how they should implement the new system. After the system was installed, management passed out report forms to measure whether the new system actually was reducing cycle time.

According to those forms, cycle time was down. But in focus groups, floor managers said the statistics weren't true—that, in fact, they had lied on the forms.

Why would they lie? Well, they said, management lied to us: They asked for our input on the new system, but we didn't see our ideas included.

Management had gathered initial feedback, but had not taken the time to explain how final decisions were made, and how that employee feedback had been used—or not used. In the absence of any explanations, employees assumed deception and therefore felt free to sabotage the company's plans. And they felt no guilt in doing so.

In this case, the company had spent $10 million on the TQM program. Its inability to work honestly with its employees made it unlikely the company would see a fair return on that investment. The cultural issues got in the way of financial performance.

Such deliberate sabotage may be the most severe consequence of keeping the truth locked up. But treating your employees as if they can't handle the truth also may induce a passive/aggressive behavior that's almost as troublesome. Thinking to themselves, "You don't care what I think," employees will respond by bringing their bodies to work, but checking their brains at the door.

Then there are the more subtle consequences of keeping the truth at bay. When people don't have a chance to express their intense feelings directly, those feelings tend to manifest themselves in other ways.

If you allow people to vent their emotions, then you can get into their brains. If they can't vent, they will act out their feelings through their behavior. But their feelings *will* get expressed, either verbally or behaviorally.

Employees will call in sick more frequently, for instance. Workers' compensation claims and lawsuits will increase. And by not offering your employees a forum to speak honestly, get answers to their questions and get it all off their chests, you will have driven up the hidden costs of your business and damaged your bottom line.

Reaping the Rewards

Speaking the unspeakable sets a tone of honesty and integrity. If you can maintain that honesty, you will continue reaping benefits.

Honesty attracts honesty. According to Kim Woods of ABN AMRO North America, "I have found that a lot of people are thinking the exact same thing, but just haven't said it. So speaking the unspeakable helps you find people who would have said the same thing if they had the nerve."

Honesty gives you valuable leverage. In times like ours, when business conditions are changing so rapidly, the "truth" can be a fleeting thing. What's true today isn't necessarily true tomorrow. The best business decision today may be a wrong move tomorrow. And that can make you look like a liar to your employees, because you have changed your position.

But if you have established a reputation for honesty and trust, you will be able to go to your workforce and say, "You know, three months ago I told you this. Now things have changed and that is no longer true. And here's why." In an environment of trust and honesty, you'll be able to make that statement and people will be more likely to accept it. If you try to do that in an atmosphere of cynicism and distrust, it won't fly.

At a company that had gone through severe downsizing, the CEO made an announcement that the layoffs were over. But just months after the announcement was made, the CEO had to reverse himself. The financial situation had changed; an unexpected market downturn and new products that weren't meeting sales expectations necessitated another round of cuts.

This company had worked hard to create an environment of trust and mutual respect between leaders and workers. When the CEO laid out the facts to the workforce, he said, "Because I promised you that there would be no more cuts, and because I have to let people go quickly, I'm going to increase the severance packages for these people." The response was phenomenal. The workforce was disappointed by the layoffs but supportive of the decision—because the CEO explained the business conditions, outlined what had happened in the marketplace, and took care of those who were let go.

Honesty is simply more productive, especially in our cynical, skeptical culture.

"People can smell a fraud in a second," says Mark Stavish of America Online. "Honesty distinguishes great leadership today." Save yourself the grief and wasted time of excessive water-cooler chatter and closed-door meetings. Be honest with your people whenever you can.

Honesty can help you attract and retain top performers. In the competition for talent today, the best and brightest workers have lots of choices about where they work. If you are the leader of a traditional company, you may not be able to let these workers wear shorts and sandals to the office, or to bring their dog to work. But you can offer them honesty as a sign of a caring environment. That really matters to people, especially the hard-on-the-outside, hopeful-on-the-inside Generation Xers.

"Caring is not an environment devoid of confrontation," says Cisco's Carl Russo. "Quite the opposite.

"If you have a pile of snot hanging out of your nose, who cares more about you: The person that comes up and says, 'Look, I don't know if you know this or not, but you've got a pile of snot hanging out of your nose'? Or the people that avoid you and for fear of hurting your feelings don't raise it?"

And with that kind of caring environment, *you can speed up your entire work process.*

Russo worked hard to create such an environment when he headed up Cerent, the company he founded that was acquired for $7 billion by Cisco in 1999. He explains: "At the end of the day, there's nothing I can do to remove the giant flashing 'CEO' sign that runs around above my head all day long. People associate that title with titular authority."

But he worked hard to gain his workers' trust. "I tried to get everyone comfortable. I didn't dress any differently than anyone else. Didn't move differently than anyone else. I was honest with everyone. I also cut up with anyone. I'd start kidding with people and get them to be comfortable with that—get them to be comfortable with taking shots back.

"And eventually they would get so comfortable that the inevitable happens: When something's bothering them one day, before they even think *not* to tell me, they tell me. They're not thinking about their mortgage and family, and the fact that I'm the boss, before they say anything to me."

Russo believes that level of trust is the key to real creativity in the workplace. "What exists in a company that feels like family is a level of safety where people actually feel safe to be themselves," he says. "And if they're feeling safe enough to be themselves then maybe, just maybe, they'll feel safe enough to be creative in public.

"And if you can get a bunch of people to exert their creativity without thinking about it, you've got something."

You've got eLeadership.

5

Make Loud Statements

THE NEW eWORLD OF SPEED AND FLEXIBILITY demands
bold moves. You need to offer employees undeniable proof
that the Industrial Age corporate culture is gone, and that
you are creating an environment for the future. The way to
do that is to blatantly and offensively break with the past
through loud statements of change, and then to reinforce
that with new, irreverent communications.

A loud statement can take many forms: speeches, meetings, personal but public actions. The key is that it comes
from the top of the organization, it generally comes at the beginning of a change effort, and it breaks the company's implicit rules.

Every company operates under a set of implicit communications rules that dictate what behavior is or is not accept-
able. Too often today there is not just a gap, but a huge gulf

between a company's explicit rhetoric and the behaviors being reinforced by the implicit rules.

For instance, a company may say, "We need you to challenge our ideas, take risks, be innovative, and play on a team." But the implicit rules tell employees: "The boss is always right. You are part of a silo, not a team. You need to cover your ass. If it's not invented here, it's not worthwhile."

As long as this gulf exists, companies will have difficulty meeting their strategic objectives. When the explicit rhetoric says one thing and the implicit rules reinforce another, employees receive inconsistent messages that cost a company time and money. Such a gulf virtually guarantees failure in this new world of speed and flexibility.

In today's world the customer is king. When employees waste their time trying to decide which of your messages to follow, they are wasting time that could be spent adding value for the customer.

As you work to make your company's rhetoric match its behavior, some of the first and most important messages must come from you, the eLeader. Your goal is to break the patterns of the past, and to encourage the behaviors needed to create an agile, honest, flexible environment. As leader, you do that in two ways.

First, you must make an ongoing, day-to-day commitment to model personally those behaviors with your words and actions. Understand you may need a coach. Chances are the behaviors that helped you get where you are today are not the behaviors you need to move into the future. You must be willing to break the rules of the past—your rules, the rules that made you successful.

The second and most powerful platform you have is a big, dramatic action or presentation that breaks the company's old rules in front of a large group of your employees. You personally must make a loud statement that things are changing at your organization—and they never will be the same again.

Educational Testing Service's Story: Erasing the Past, Penciling in the Future

Not many organizations can institute tough changes and simultaneously—and in less than two years—turn a deficit into a surplus. That's what Educational Testing Service managed to do, by making a carefully thought-out loud statement of change and communicating it well.

ETS is the premier organization developing standardized testing for the nation's college and graduate school network. But in 1998 it found itself in need of pressing changes.

Three years earlier, ETS had made a serious and necessary commitment to turn some of its paper-and-pencil testing systems into computer products. But the project was unexpectedly expensive. ETS is a nonprofit organization, but it began to run a deficit and eat into its reserve monies—at a time when it needed to invest more in R&D. In addition, the push for rapid computerization left some employees feeling that ETS's pristine reputation for quality was in danger. Plus, everyone's workload was changing.

ETS employees were overworked and unhappy. "Computer-based testing was taking up all the air, all the money, all the talent. It put enormous stress on the system," says Sharon Robinson, senior vice-president and chief operating officer. "Employees were feeling very uneasy about their professional integrity and were worried about continuing to produce the quality that is ETS's cachet."

When leadership agreed that the organization had to change, they knew it would be tough. ETS embarked on "a cost-management effort including getting our compensation costs in line—to make them more disciplined and predictable because we had to make sure our products stayed at a competitive price point," Robinson says.

The ETS plan forced the company to speak about a key unspeakable—money—and talk about it publicly. This was an academic culture that talked quality, not dollars. "The mantra always was: 'Do you want it cheaper or do you want it done right?'" Robinson says.

In addition, the proposed changes in employee compensation and benefits hit several of the company's sacred cows. No longer would academics and test developers be paid more than employees who handled such functions as technology, client management, and marketing; in a tight job market, the company needed to pay more to successfully recruit for those functions. ETS also ditched a system that paid more for seniority, instituting a pay-for-performance plan instead.

To deliver the loud statements of change, ETS leadership launched a three-part campaign called "Straight Talk." The top three ETS leaders held meetings with all of the company's employees, one hundred to two hundred at a time. Reaching everyone required holding three separate sessions, each with twelve meetings, three weeks apart—a real commitment of time.

The first component of the road show: sharing the business case for change—"an in-depth and candid representation of the competitive situation within our industry and also within the labor market," Robinson says. To convince everyone that change was necessary, leadership laid out all the company's costs and recent spending patterns to show why continuing in that fashion "would undermine our basic existence," she says.

Then came the second component, in which the three leaders discussed the changes in compensation plans, and the third component, a presentation that dealt with changes in employee benefits.

By the time "Straight Talk" was finished, the three leaders—then-CEO Nancy Cole and CFO Frank Gatti in addition to COO Robinson—met as a team with each ETS employee three times. Each meeting was hosted by an independent journalist; a no-holds-barred question-and-answer session was included. Employees could follow up with additional questions on the company's intranet. In addition, an electronic newsletter kept everyone posted with important information, while quarterly meetings kept top managers in the loop.

Despite all the personal attention, there was a lot of resistance to the changes. "When the dust settled, frankly I was surprised the company was still standing," Robinson says.

But not only is the company still standing—it's thriving.

The plan called for ETS to eliminate its deficit within three years. But less than two years after the "Straight Talk" campaign introduced the changes, ETS was back in the black—and getting ready to fund two new product ideas.

Part of the secret was respecting the history of the organization, and appealing to employees' pride and sense of ownership. "In our cost-cutting message, we said this would not happen as a result of some grand scheme crafted at the top of the company," Robinson says. "This would only happen if everyone at every desk questioned every expense. I think they thought, 'This is ETS—we're not going to let it fail.'"

And after the first year, despite much resistance and many complaints, "They had managed to cut the deficit way more than we'd expected, while the service levels stayed up," she says.

To celebrate, ETS management scheduled a Staff Appreciation Day. While employees celebrated with cupcakes and punch, Cole, Robinson, and Gatti went out to the various ETS buildings and personally shook hands with each employee. A separate letter of appreciation went out from Cole.

It was a tough, emotional campaign, but given the results, says Robinson, "I don't know how we could have achieved what we did as fast as we did. If you move into a leadership role in an organization, you must embrace the responsibility of making it better.

"I'm very proud of what we've accomplished."

It Has to Start with You

People follow people. They don't follow blueprints or words on a piece of paper. Particularly in the uncertain atmosphere surrounding change, people want the comfort of following a leader.

An eLeader's job is to lead the charge, reinforce the importance of what the company is doing, and rally the troops. A loud statement can do all three things.

One of my favorite leadership stories comes from William Shakespeare's retelling of the story of Henry V, king of England. Henry and his poorly armed, exhausted, and over-matched army are preparing for battle with the French army. As his troops head to the battlefield, Henry reaches deep inside to deliver a speech that makes his men's hearts pound with pride, hope, and commitment:

> If we are mark'd to die, we are enow
> To do our country loss; and if to live,
> The fewer men, the greater share of honor. . . .
> Rather proclaim it, Westmoreland, through my host,
> That he which hath no stomach to this fight,
> Let him depart; his passport shall be made
> And crowns for convoy put into his purse:
> We would not die in that man's company
> That fears his fellowship to die with us.
> This day is called the feast of Crispian:
> He that outlives this day, and comes safe home,
> Will stand a tip-toe when this day is named,
> And rouse him at the name of Crispian.
> He that shall live this day, and see old age,
> Will yearly on the vigil feast his neighbours,
> And say 'Tomorrow is Saint Crispian:'
> Then will he strip his sleeve and show his scars.

And say, "These wounds I had on Crispian's day. . . . "
We few, we happy few, we band of brothers;
For he today that sheds his blood with me
Shall be my brother; be he ne'er so vile,
This day shall gentle his condition:
And gentlemen in England now a-bed
Shall think themselves accursed they were not here,
And hold their manhoods cheap whiles any speaks
That fought with us upon Saint Crispian's day.

(Henry V, Act 4, Scene 3)

Henry made a loud statement. He offered "safe passage" for the bottom 20%. He spoke the unspeakable truth, admitting that he, the king, and his soldiers probably were going to die on the battlefield. He broke the implicit rules of the time by proclaiming that he and his men were brothers—and then modeled the desired behavior himself by leaving behind his kingly privileges, mounting his horse, and joining in the battle. He painted his vision of the future, his prediction of this battle's importance for England. And then he told his men what was in it for them: Someday, they'd be able to show off their scars and tell their grandchildren that they were participants in this battle that had such momentous import for England.

Of course, the results are the stuff of legend. At Shakespeare's Battle of Agincourt, Henry's army suffers almost no losses and defeats the French army five times its size.

You may not be as inspirational as Henry V, and especially Shakespeare's version of him. Few of us are. But you can find your own ways of making loud statements that inspire your workforce to face an uncertain future.

Remember that a loud statement must begin with a statement of personal commitment. If you don't believe in what you are selling, no one else will either—no matter how loud your statement. On the other hand, if you really believe and you are really trying, people will give you credit and support even if you make mistakes and your results aren't perfect.

Nine other elements should be considered when making a loud statement of change. You may want or need to:

- Respect the past
- Present your vision of the future
- Speak the unspeakables
- Break the implicit rules
- Slaughter the sacred cows
- Model and reinforce the new behaviors
- Make a personal commitment
- Orchestrate communications
- Follow through

A loud statement of change may accomplish one or several of these tasks. If it is part of a larger meeting, remember that the loud statement will encompass not only words, but also the setting and the way the words are delivered.

When Nextera orchestrates a meeting that is designed to make a loud statement of change, we consider everything from the way the stage is set up to the way the employees are greeted. We want to create an experience that makes a loud statement. Everything about the meeting can send the message that this is not the same company anymore.

For one company whose top leaders had acted as if stuck in different silos, we made sure those leaders were on stage together for virtually the entire meeting. For another, we held the big meeting in the executive parking lot—a clear signal that something big and unexpected would be happening.

In these two cases, from the moment employees walked in the message was: This is a different company.

Respect the Past

It sounds odd, but when making a loud statement of change, the first thing a leader must address is people's investment in the past.

Dedicated employees have spent time and energy getting the company where it is. Their efforts using the old ways of doing business have been very successful—sometimes for years. Their experience and knowledge can be valuable assets in the future. And it's not their fault that frequently the "old rules" are the only rules they've known.

The old behaviors aren't wrong; they just don't work today. Times have changed, markets have changed, competition has changed. New behaviors are needed to meet these new challenges.

So before you begin talking boldly about leaving the past, take a moment to pay homage to the people, processes, and protocols that made your company successful. Make sure people know that without their hard work in the past, the company might not be in a position even to consider how to succeed in the future.

You may choose to pay your respects through a newsletter, a memo, or face-to-face acknowledgments. When they host a large employee meeting to make a loud statement of change, many companies choose to begin the proceedings with a videotaped history of the company and its achievements.

To open an employee meeting designed to discuss changes, one company prepared a video that not only outlined the corporate history and milestones, but also found in that history the roots of the new values being introduced.

Another large industrial company was forced to make a tough decision about its original and most loved facility. This was a company that did not publicly discuss negative actions. But to respect the past, this company broke that corporate rule to honor a beloved facility's place in company history.

In a story for its corporate video newsmagazine, the company's communications department sketched the location's history. Then the former facility general manager discussed the difficult situation: how market changes had forced a series of increasingly severe cutbacks, until a friendly buyer appeared on the scene to save the facility from closing, and save many community jobs as well.

A third company was forced to make the difficult decision to close one of its oldest plants and outsource work. It was traumatic for the plant employees, many of whom had worked there more than twenty-five years. And for the rest of the employees, closing this plant was a sign that the company was in serious trouble. To deal with the employees' emotions, the company leadership laid out the case for change, gave everyone as much notice as possible, and offered generous severance packages or retention-bonuses.

On the day the plant was closing, the company president visited the site to host a closing ceremony. And the company newsletter continued to update employees about their former colleagues.

The sensitive way the plant closing was handled kept employee morale high and helped prevent turnover in other parts of the company. During plant shutdowns, workers' compensation claims tend to increase; in this situation, those claims actually decreased.

Tuning in to employees' connection with the past will help soothe any feelings of loss, allow people to express their grief, and clear the path for change.

Everyone at your company may know you need to change. What may not be clear is the link between the successes of the past and the changes that will ensure success in the future. It's your job to provide that transition.

Present Your Vision

You are about ready to make a loud statement of change—to break with the past. But where are you taking your company? What is your goal? Why should your employees be interested in learning new systems, embracing new behaviors, and leaving their old level of comfort?

You can answer all those questions by effectively presenting your vision of the company's future. You want to paint a picture that is exciting and relevant. You also want to help your employees understand that you wouldn't be asking them to change unless it was important. Share the case for change, and give them a strong reason to support the effort.

Like Henry V at Agincourt, you personally must be willing to do what you ask from your workers. If you're asking them to stick with the company through the change process, you need to tell them you also are in it for the long haul.

You also need to tell the staff why their efforts matter, and how this company can make a difference in the world. That statement is particularly relevant to Generation X and Y employees, who really want to know that their work matters.

As we have discussed in earlier chapters, vision is one of the tools the best-run eCompanies have used to their great advantage in attracting the best talent and keeping those workers motivated. Whether it's Steve Jobs in the early days of Apple Computer or Steve Case at America Online, the great high-tech leaders have made a passionate case for their companies' role in fundamentally altering modern life.

"People at AOL really believe they're changing the world," says senior VP Mark Stavish. "That's not something I've experienced in other big corporations." That fervor starts with AOL founder Steve Case, who through good times and bad has been a relentless missionary for his company's importance in the world.

Brad Keywell of Starbelly.com says part of the challenge of an Internet company is boiling down its vision to an "elevator pitch"—being able to explain the company's story during a single elevator ride. Frankly, I think that's a useful concept for traditional companies as well; as Keywell says, if you don't have a corporate vision that concise and potent, "shame on you."

To keep his company's vision fresh and alive, Keywell hosts a weekly vision meeting: a brown-bag breakfast where Starbelly employees "talk about how all this started and why we're here and where it's going."

"We don't sort of *hope* that everyone finds inspiration," he says. "It's been my job and my partners' job to have inspiration—from the beginning. Then it's my job to pass it on very tenderly, through lots of time and handling, to everyone else. If they don't get it, take more time. It's worth the time to pass on the inspiration.

"If someone can really grasp what it is that started this company—what the nucleus of our idea was—they will do their job better, no matter what that job is."

When Jimmy de Castro had to make widespread changes at AMFM, he told his managers this was a chance "to change the face of radio."

Herb Kelleher for years successfully has rallied the employees of Southwest Airlines to work for "freedom of the airways."

Andy Rosenfield, the leader of UNext.com, Cardean University's new online MBA program, calls for "the democratization of education."

In his speech to kick off the new millennium, Roger Brossy of Nextera's Sibson said, "I know that, together, we can reinvent consulting. I know we can help our clients remain strong and competitive in this New Economy."

As you make a loud statement of change and then lead the

change effort, use the "vision thing" to inspire commitment from your workforce. Tap their desire to change the world; do it with a solid business case and you will win both their heads and their hearts.

Speak the Unspeakables

Henry V's speech preceding the Battle of Agincourt was successful and powerful not just because he was a great speaker. Henry had done his homework.

In Shakespeare's version, Henry spends the night before the battle preparing for the big moment. He disguises himself and circulates among the troops. Moving from campfire to campfire, he listens to the medieval version of water-cooler chatter—his soldiers' unspeakable fears about the day to come. After hearing those honest and painful concerns, Henry delivers a speech—his loud statement—designed to tackle those fears and help the troops rise above them.

We've discussed the importance of speaking the unspeakables to your workforce. Your job is to really listen to the unspeakables and deal with them. It's an important part of your loud statement of change.

Loud statement: The biggest unspeakable topic at CCH was the fear that the company wouldn't survive a transition from print publisher to software publisher. CEO Oakleigh Thorne, the fifth generation of his family to run CCH, looked that big unspeakable issue straight in the eye. He filmed an internal "commercial," which ran on big screens during the company's all-employee videoconference, in which he proclaimed to all CCH staffers, "I made myself a promise: The ship's not going down on my watch."

A loud statement should tackle directly the unspeakable subjects—whether that is, for instance, a lack of confidence in leadership, a doomed feeling about the company's future, or hostility toward certain work processes. Only by publicly discussing those unspeakable thoughts can an eLeader get them out of the way of the change effort.

Break the Implicit Rules

Every company operates with sets of rules. Some are explicit, printed in employee handbooks or discussed in orientation sessions. Others, however, are *implicit* rules—the company's unwritten ways of communicating and understood norms of behavior.

Does your company live by any of these typical implicit rules?

- Don't question authority.
- Form is more important than substance.
- The boss always makes the final decision.
- We don't admit our mistakes.
- It's better to be cautious than to take a risk and fail.
- No one laughs at the senior leadership team in public.
- New mothers are bad risks for promotions.

- "Regular" employees are not welcome on the "executive floor."
- The size of your office reflects your importance at the company.

These sorts of implicit rules are roadblocks to change. Frequently protected by the bottom 20% of the workforce, implicit rules trip up the middle 60%, causing them to hesitate and to hide the truth. Instead of acting in the best interests of the company, they use implicit rules to guide their behavior.

Loud statement: Grainger, North America's largest distributor of maintenance, repair, and operating supplies, wanted to enact a major cultural change, to bring its work environment into the twenty-first century. This catalogue and bricks-and-mortar company saw the Internet looming large. In 1996, a small group of senior Grainger executives met and began formulating a list of values they wanted to establish for the company. Led by CEO Richard Keyser, these executives were committed to living the values, not merely engraving them on plaques. Those values would help create an environment to succeed in this changing world and serve as the foundation of the company's business decisions and strategic plan.

The values were fairly typical of the characteristics any large bureaucratic company might want to cultivate in making the transition to the eWorld:

- Agility: The company wanted to move more quickly and resourcefully.
- Empowerment and Accountability: It wanted to

give employees more responsibility while demanding more accountability.

- Ethics and Integrity: It wanted to commit to fairness and honesty in all aspects of its business.
- Teamwork: It wanted to find ways to encourage a collegial environment.
- Learning: It wanted to be an organization open to honest criticism and learning.
- Having fun: It wanted its employees to balance their personal and professional lives, and enjoy themselves.

While top executives were drafting the values, Grainger simultaneously but independently was planning a meeting of 450 top managers. That meeting seemed a great opportunity to discuss the new values, get broader employee input, and also bring the values to life through the way the meeting was conducted.

"We saw this as our chance to make such a loud statement about where we were headed that everyone would listen," said Todd Cook, the Grainger executive who coordinated the meeting and is now an independent consultant.

Implicit Versus Explicit:
How Communications Rules Affect Behavior

On the next page is a typical list comparing the implicit communications rules at an organization, and the types of behaviors they encourage, to the revised, explicit rules and the behaviors they elicit.

OLD, IMPLICIT COMMUNICATIONS RULES	RESULTING BEHAVIORS	NEW, EXPLICIT COMMUNICATIONS RULES	DESIRED BEHAVIORS
Do not question authority	Leaders are respected and their opinions are accepted at face value	Challenge ideas	Ideas and sound thinking are respected and encouraged
Confrontation is unhealthy, insensitive, and disrespectful	Avoid confrontation and friction	Confrontation is healthy, sensitive, and respectful	Interactions can involve productive confrontation
Complaining is acceptable; doing nothing about a problem is OK	Reactive: crisis mentality	Acknowledging problems is good, but we also must develop solutions and take action	Proactive: People anticipate situations and approach them as opportunities
It's important that the individual get credit for an idea	Ideas are not shared for fear of losing individual recognition and rewards. Silo mentality	Sharing ideas and teaming up are good. It's important that the team and the company succeed	People are sharing, challenging, and developing ideas; teams and groups receive recognition
The customer is king	Reactive fire fighting	The customer is a business partner	People seek proactive identification of opportunities and interactive problem solving
Good performance is treated almost the same as mediocre performance	Lack of interest in improving team or individual results	Good performance is rewarded and celebrated	Consistent support for and interest in improving performance

This meeting, tagged "Painting Our Future," would indeed be a loud statement of change—or, as it turned out, a barrage of loud statements.

The key to the meeting's power and success was that Cook and his team had identified many of the company's implicit rules. Virtually every facet of the meeting was designed to reinforce the newly codified values and break the implicit rules of the past.

"To show how we were changing, this meeting would break, very publicly, with the old rules and policies," Cook said. "So in planning the meeting, as soon as anyone told me a rule, we'd find a way to break it.

"We especially tried to focus on the implicit rules that were not in alignment with our new values."

The changes were apparent as soon as the attendees gathered at the meeting site, and the surprises continued during the two-day affair. Here are some samples:

Old rule: Form is more important than function.

Rulebreaker: Hand-drawn nametags. Rather than the company's longstanding standard-issue badges, everyone was asked to draw his own nametag with bright colored markers and crayons.

Reinforced the new values of: resourcefulness and having fun.

Old rule: Hierarchy is important.

Rulebreaker: Identical meeting T-shirts that broke down distinctions of rank. To reinforce the message that the senior leadership was just a bunch of guys, too, an outside facilitator introduced the nine Grainger leaders with a slide show of photos—of the execs as babies, with their families, or in funny situations. The videos broke the ice and made the executives appear human.

The executives sat in a semicircle on the stage, in directors' chairs. From the minute employees walked in the door, they knew this was a different company: The stage was covered with paint cans and brushes and a big empty canvas. Although the meeting was being taped, to prevent it looking like just another meeting, the wires from the electrical equipment were exposed.

Reinforced the new values of: teamwork, balancing personal and professional lives, having fun, and moving quickly—without regard to hierarchy.

Old rule: You can't question corporate decisions. In fact, those who stir up trouble will be punished.

Rulebreaker: A discussion of the company's unaskable questions. "We'd asked everyone coming to the meeting to send us a question that he'd never dare to ask in public," Cook said. The outside facilitator led the discussion of the top ten unaskable questions and pressed the executive team for honest, useful responses.

Reinforced the new values of: responsibility and accountability, and the commitment to honesty.

Old rule: Leadership meets behind closed doors.

Rulebreaker: At one point in the meeting, the senior leaders met to discuss some of the meeting's revelations—in the middle of everyone, with microphones on. "It was like they were in a fish bowl," said meeting coordinator Cook.

Reinforced the new values of: honesty, teamwork, and learning.

In one part of the meeting, the team of senior executives made a unique presentation. Each executive was responsible for introducing one of the new values by explaining why that value was personally important. He told a story of how he had successfully lived the value, and then told a story of how he had done something counter to the value.

The executives were given their instructions only the night before the meeting. Because they weren't allowed to use a speechwriter, they spoke without notes, from the heart. The stories were very personal and emotional, full of confessions and intimate details.

"The response of the audience was overwhelming," Cook said. "Seeing the importance these things have on the senior guys was incredibly powerful.

"This group of executives had great intentions to help the company change and really live up to those values. They put a lot of themselves into this effort, to start off on the right foot."

During the meeting, Grainger had hired an artist to circulate among the participants and create abstract illustrations that brought the six values to life. Employees were asked to choose the representations they liked. Reflecting the meeting's "Painting Our Future" theme, the artist painted a collage with all six symbols included. The picture hung on the stage during the rest of the meeting.

Grainger got a huge boost in employee morale out of

the meeting. Afterward, cards listing the new corporate values were passed out to all employees. To this day, the values—including the artist's representation—occupy a prominent place in corporate communications, from posters in the offices to a presence on the company's website.

The implicit rules can produce behaviors that can defeat the whole change effort.

You need to make the implicit rules explicit in order to break them, and then write new explicit rules that the company actually will follow. After you catalogue your company's implicit rules, you must design a loud statement that specifically breaks those rules.

Loud statement: One of the unwritten rules at this midwestern company was that senior leadership wasn't held accountable for company performance. At a managers' meeting addressing the need to change, several members of the senior leadership team performed a skit that made fun of "pass the buck" behaviors. They dressed up as Goldilocks and the Three Bears and pretended to be in a management meeting where no one would make a decision. One executive said, "It's too hot!" A second said, "It's too cold!" In subsequent speeches, leadership took responsibility for the company's performance and addressed other inefficient work practices.

After the leadership skit, the employees were divided into teams. Each team was asked to create a skit that took aim at a behavior that needed to change. Because top leaders had done such a good job making fun of their inefficient behaviors, the teams felt free to be extremely creative in taking on other troublesome habits.

Be prepared to meet with resistance, especially with rules that have become entrenched. You may have to make a first loud statement and then continue to hammer home the theme to really change the behavior.

Loud statement: Marks & Spencer, the famed British retailer, is going through a businesswide transition. "We want to become an integrated multichannel retailer," says Keith Bogg, director of U.K. retailing, e-commerce. "We want to focus totally on the customer and say: 'You can order it any way you like—store, catalogue, Internet—and we'll deliver it where you like, to home, office, wherever.'" Its new focus has resulted in changes in jobs and in the skills required to perform many of those jobs. M&S made its loud statement last year by asking its top managers to reapply for their jobs—or a new job if they preferred. Every job had new qualifications, and people had to prove they had the skills for the future by undergoing testing and an interview. That an employee had a job didn't mean he would get to keep it.

Slaughter the Sacred Cows

While you are identifying and breaking the implicit rules of your company, you're almost sure to stumble on a few sacred cows—the symbols of the old ways of doing business. Slaughter those sacred cows.

These can be true symbols, such as favorite projects, office space, and dress codes.

Loud statement: At one company, we took the time clocks into the employee parking lot and literally smashed them. Two points were made eloquently: Both management and workers needed to pay more attention to performance than merely to the time spent on the job. And management trusted workers to budget their time and get the job done—on their own.

Loud statement: The division head had worked personally to construct an elaborate organizational chart, and defied the company CEO to put it in place. It was his baby. What Sibson found in focus groups was that the organizational chart had become a barrier to success for this division, which accounted for 70 percent of the company's revenues. Under its complex reporting relationships, no one was accountable for decision-making. But it was seen as the boss's sacred cow, so no one challenged it; instead, people merely worked around it.

When presented with the results of our focus group interviews, the division head owned up to the problem. He assembled a committee of his top 20% performers and had them spend one weekend working out a new organizational chart; no one could leave the meeting until it was done. The division head then went back to the CEO, admitted he'd made a mistake, and got approval to install the new system. His actions served as testimony to his commitment to change.

Sacred cows also can be traditional, revered ways of doing business: policies that have been in place for years or assumptions that the business needs to operate in a certain way.

Loud statement: Ernst & Young has a well-earned reputation and has won many awards for exemplary customer service. Yet the Lake Michigan division of the company found in an internal survey that its employees felt slighted. They felt E&Y's customer focus left little time to take care of employees.

To show its two thousand employees how much it did care about them and appreciate their efforts, management of the Lake Michigan area planned a campaign called "People Add Value." To launch the campaign, the company took on a sacred cow.

"When you look at the auditing and tax business, the busiest time of the year is from January through March," says Ray McGowan, partner and director of human resources for E&Y's Lake Michigan area. "We thought: What if we were to have a huge party for everyone just to say thank you and planned it right in the middle of that very busiest time of year?"

The company reserved Chicago's House of Blues restaurant/club for a party on February 19, 1999. Everyone in the region was invited; the company even rented buses and a train to convey people from the Wisconsin and Michigan branch offices.

There were food stations everywhere, plus an open bar and a DJ. Everyone got a pair of sunglasses when they walked in. Because a second goal of the party was to show management as more approachable, the three top managers dressed up as the Blues Brothers—hats, sunglasses, white shirts, skinny ties, and so forth—and began their entrance from the club's top level. They danced through the crowd to the main stage.

When the area managing partner took the stage, he said only two things: "Thank you for all you do for our firm. And beginning Monday, we are going to business casual dress year-round." The three leaders then shed their coats and ties, and the room went crazy.

More than a thousand people came to the party. Hundreds were still there when the party was scheduled to end, at 10:00 P.M.

The party and the statement it made about E&Y's new priorities were such a huge success that the Lake Michigan Area held a second one in February 2000.

In your push for a way to let your workforce know that real change is on the way, find your own sacred cow and get rid of it as publicly as possible.

Reinforce the New Behaviors

Speaking the unspeakables, breaking implicit rules, and slaughtering sacred cows all are aimed at getting rid of past behaviors. The other part of a loud statement is designed to reinforce the new, desired behaviors.

If you are hosting a change kickoff meeting, plan some contest or device that simulates the behaviors required to implement your new strategic direction. These devices help people learn by doing, and gets them thinking about doing things differently.

When Grainger introduced its new corporate values, it had its 450 managers work to symbolize the values by drawing pictures.

Loud statement: AMFM had made the announcement that it was reorganizing its workforce to change the way radio time was sold to sponsors. CEO Jimmy de Castro and his team made the point that the rules of the radio marketplace had changed forever. Those who sold time for stations needed to be more strategic, more focused.

The kickoff meeting was set in a downtown Chicago bowling alley. Near the end of the meeting, we divided the attendees into two groups and asked them to bowl. But we changed the rules: Rather than pushing for sheer power—knocking down all ten pins for a strike— teams were asked to do one focused thing: Knock down the 7 pin.

Predictably, one of the teams went out and bowled their hearts out in conventional fashion. But the other team huddled and figured out a strategy: The most efficient way to knock down the 7 pin was to walk down the gutter and push it down with their hands.

The second team won, strongly and cleverly making

the point to everyone at the meeting that the new marketplace required reconsidering at all the old rules—and sometimes turning them upside down.

Loud statement: For another client, we also used a game to show how this company, whose employees tended to work in silos, could benefit in the marketplace by collaborating. We divided the meeting attendees into two teams, and each team into four smaller groups. The trick was that everyone had to play the game blindfolded—a metaphor for the difficult market conditions this company was fighting.

One of the eight smaller groups figured out a way around the rules: They cut holes in their blindfolds. Thinking themselves very clever, they watched everyone else struggling, and waited to reveal their trick until the end of the game. It seemed like a perfect competitive advantage.

The problem was that they didn't share the secret with the other groups on their team. The other team won the overall match.

The lesson about the damage that happens to a company when working in silos rather than in a collaborative, knowledge-sharing environment was lost on no one.

In addition to reinforcing the new desired behaviors at big meetings like these, you'll want to continue the reinforcement back at company headquarters.

A venture capitalist I admire tells the story of one of the Internet companies he works with that didn't support the new behaviors it espoused: The company had grown to a point where, like many Internet start-ups, it needed outside management help. It turned to an industry veteran from a large high-tech company and named him chief operating officer. "His job was to be the tough guy, the guy who gets the trains to run on time," said the financier.

Unfortunately, he continued, "The culture here nearly killed the new COO. That's because the company founder talked the talk of change, but wasn't willing to take the actions necessary to support the change agent."

A month or two after the new COO had started, there was a big blowup between him and the chief technology officer, who threatened to quit. Rather than mediate the situation, the founder used the opportunity to approach the board and suggested the COO be removed. "It was a classic case of the organization trying to kill the change agent," the venture capitalist said. And, of course, it's a classic case of not reinforcing behaviors correctly.

Luckily, this board was smart enough to take a closer look. They kept the COO, moved the founder into a more ceremonial role at the company, and began the search for a new CEO.

Make a Personal Commitment

As eLeader you are committed to change. By making a loud statement, you have taken a visible role in the change effort. But you can fire off a smaller but very powerful loud statement by making a personal commitment that shows just how much you value and believe in the change effort.

Frequently that means putting your money where your mouth is.

Loud statement: When, in its early days, yesmail.com came precariously close to not making its payroll, CEO Dave Tolmie quietly wrote a three-hundred-thousand-dollar check to cover the amount due to employees. Although only his senior team initially knew what he was doing, what a powerful statement that kind of gesture made about Tolmie's faith in his company.

Loud statement: Embroiled in trying to change a dangerously troubled company, and criticized for not being a leader, the division head of a Fortune 50 company took all his available cash and invested it all in the company's plummeting stock. And he told people he was doing it.

Loud statement: Similarly, Nextera's Sibson president, Roger Brossy, used the occasion of a partners' meeting to announce that he was buying additional stock of the parent company, Nextera. Brossy had just watched the partners arrive at several decisions critical to the future, and wanted to emphasize just how much he believed in those decisions. His comment: "I'm a builder. I'm a believer. I'm an investor."

Remember, people follow people. Your strong and visible commitment to your company lends credibility to the change effort and reassurance to your employees.

Orchestrate Communications

Your change effort may begin with a loud statement at a kickoff meeting. But that meeting probably won't include your entire workforce. To make sure the loud statement is echoed throughout the organization, you must orchestrate a strategic communications plan that gets a synchronized message delivered in a timely fashion. It not only must give the information that people need, but also must be done in a way that reinforces behaviors for the future.

We'll discuss many more communications tactics in the next chapter, but one important facet that frequently can be overlooked is one you should see to yourself. You should make sure your senior managers get any executive coaching they might need to accurately communicate your message of change and to actively participate in the effort.

Most top managers have good presentation skills. This is not about that; it's about modeling and encouraging the right behaviors. Your senior leadership team must understand that communication is more than just the dissemination of information; it is the reinforcement of behavior—behaviors that drive strategy. The executives must see how their own behavior and their communication style reinforces or defeats necessary behaviors of their employees.

If a team is not well versed in behavior-driven communications, consider training them in how to talk to their workers one-on-one. If baby boom managers are being asked to tune in to their Generation X employees, perhaps they need tips on eliciting and encouraging feedback.

Loud statement: In early 1999, Wachovia Bank wanted to increase customer enrollment in its Internet banking service. When the division was moved under executive vice-president Lawrence Baxter, he told the team that he wanted them to enroll five hundred thousand Internet customers by the end of 2000.

"There was dead silence," Baxter remembers. The team believed such a goal wasn't possible, but they didn't tell that to Baxter. Instead, "what I got was a lot of foot-dragging," he says. "I began to realize no one was doing what I had asked them to do."

Soon he called in the person who managed the overall process. When questioned, she recited a litany of reasons why the five hundred thousand goal was impossible. Rather than shut her down, get angry, or order her to do it anyway, Baxter went through the entire list with his manager, one by one, saying, "Let's find a solution for each one."

At that point, he says, the group manager "marched off to her troops and said, 'Well, I guess he's really serious about this number. We have to get it.'" Someone on the team suggested naming the goal the "Digital 500"—Baxter embraced that and used it as a rallying cry. "It provided them with something to work from that was fun and exciting," he says. "It was like, once you tell the troops which hill to conquer, they're incredibly good. I understand now why people have a vision to structure their thinking and their energy."

Behaviors must be pushed down into the organization. They can't just remain at the top. As you train your top people and perhaps also that next tier of managers, make sure they have materials to use to take the change message to people who might not have been at the kickoff meeting. Help the team structure an experience for their department, division, or office, with meeting plans, videos, or written materials. And provide them with ongoing support so that your loud statement of change does not prove a one-time event.

Make sure you don't waste your personal efforts at change—arm your lieutenants with the right tools to cascade the learnings and information through your organization.

Follow Through

Delivering a loud statement of change is only the beginning. You are making a commitment to real organizational change. You have publicly proclaimed that things will be different. Now you must make sure that you follow through on the personal part of that commitment.

One of my favorite stories about how effective CEOs can be in following through and reinforcing the message of change occurred when Oakleigh Thorne and I worked together at CCH.

In the process of reengineering CCH—transforming its business from printing to software—Oakleigh had to oversee many difficult decisions. At one point it became clear that the company would have to shut down parts of its print production facilities, including a plant in New Jersey.

In a Friday afternoon meeting, we discussed the fact that a year and a half earlier, when CCH had begun the change process with its all-employee videoconference, the printers in New Jersey had asked Oakeigh if the company planned to shut down their plant. He answered by telling them that he honestly didn't know, but that if the decision was made to shut them down, he would tell them first.

Oakleigh was a true eLeader. He got on a plane and made sure he was at the plant before the first shift began at 6:00 A.M. Monday. He began telling the printers the news as they arrived at work—before the plant management even arrived at work. Simultaneously CCH sent out an internal letter informing the rest of the company.

As a result of his action and honesty, CCH was able to shut down that plant without a hitch—no sabotage, no disruptions to customer service. It still serves as a great story about the necessity and power of personally following through on your commitment to change.

A Word of Warning

A loud statement can be extremely powerful. But its power becomes dangerous if a company is not committed to continuing the change effort.

If a company makes a loud statement of change and doesn't reinforce it behaviorally, its words and actions will not match. It will do more harm than good. A loud statement done well sets a very high expectation for real change. If leadership holds the meeting but no day-to-day behavior changes, and the implicit rules stay intact, the letdown among those who attended the meeting is amazing. The anger is enormous. And frankly, that company's leadership will end up in a situation that is worse than if they had done nothing at all.

A consultant friend of mine has worked on and off over the past decade with a large, respected company that has engineered three different change kickoff meetings during that time. Each of the meetings followed the right rules: It was led by the CEO, addressed implicit rules and problem subjects, suggested and supported new behaviors, and promised more change to come.

But after each meeting, the company's leadership—for whatever reason—did not follow up on the initiative. They went back to business as usual. There was no change in the company's implicit rules. There was no ongoing communication to reinforce the behaviors necessary for change.

"It is now to the point where the employees at that company now laugh at the notion of change," my friend says. "They have no faith in management."

Make sure your loud statement doesn't backfire on you.

Loud Statements . . . and Exclamation Points

Some eLeaders make their loud statements at big, orchestrated meetings with hundreds of employees present. But others speak loudly through small actions.

Lisa White is president of pointpathbank, the online bank launched in 2000 by Synovus Financial Corp. A sixteen-year Synovus employee, she was tapped to head the team developing and introducing the Internet bank—largely because of her leadership skills.

White directs the fewer than twenty people who have been working on pointpathbank. It's a collection of Synovus veterans and high-tech/business specialists recruited from the outside world.

Not only must she create a new banking product for this $12 billion financial services company, but White also is busy creating a model for Synovus, which for the past few years has been recognized as one of *Fortune* magazine's top ten places to work in America. Can a company with 112 years of history and more than ten thousand employees adjust to the New Economy environment?

"This is so important to the future of our company that we have to do things a bit differently than we've done in the past," White says. The pointpathbank team works in the same building, but completely separate from the parent company. "We've given them all free rein to go out and create and design without being encumbered by the traditional processes and red tape that really slow business down—and have made it very difficult to operate in the high-tech world we live in today."

She says it's worked well "99 percent of the time" and allowed the start-up to make the very quick decisions its business demands.

She and Synovus know that certain behaviors—speed and agility of thought, creativity, teamwork, accountability, and willingness to make fast decisions—are needed to make this division succeed. As she's making sure her people have the necessary freedom to move fast, White is trying hard to create a work environment that supports the new work behaviors.

"I'm looking for a new way to do things, not my way or the old Synovus way. . . . We're moving at such a quick speed that there's not a lot of time to get caught up in those old traditional ways of looking at things," she says.

But White is walking a fine line: keeping the best of the Synovus culture while encouraging independent thought. Supporting a fast-paced environment but watching that her team does not get burned out by too much hard work. She tries hard to keep it all balanced.

Her group works in teams, and moves off site when they need to really focus. Knowing that these people are working long, start-up hours, she tries to be a flexible boss. "I have a couple of people who like to come in late; I want them to do that," she says. But at the same time, she says, "It's important that as their leader, they don't see me down here every night at 10:00 or 11:00 P.M. When you get your life out of balance, everything else starts to fall apart."

White leads by example. She makes a point of leaving by 6:30 each night unless necessary, to be with her husband and two children. She leaves the office during the day to go to school plays and on field trips. "I have to get my work done, too," she says. "But it makes for a well-balanced life and a happier place here at work when you can accomplish personal things as well."

She also "gets the broom out" and encourages her staff to leave at reasonable hours to help avoid burnout—even if they only go home to work more, she says, at least they're getting a change of scenery.

She does little things to keep her team motivated and make sure they're aware how much she appreciates their long hours. She sends notes and restaurant gift certificates to her staff's spouses to thank them for sacrificing family time.

Two weeks after Blair Carnahan was hired as pointpathbank's director of business development, White gave him a raise. She had reevaluated his role, found that he was earning less than the industry average, and decided to bring him up to a competitive level. Her team also was given year-end bonuses similar to those of Synovus's more senior employees, to recognize their hard work and, it was hoped, keep them on the pointpathbank team.

Like the best leaders, she also is passionate about her new bank's mission. "Creating change is hard," she says. "We are changing the inner workings of a bank. But I'm really charged up about the opportunity pointpathbank gives Synovus to go national and explore new geographical footprints.

"It's a risk for the company and for me, but if you're not taking any risks, you're just sitting back being complacent with life. I decided that I was going to take this risk, and if I fail, I'll be able to say that I gave it my best shot—and I'm going to be a better person, and a better leader, for the experience."

Are You Ready to Close the Creed-Deed Gap?

Being an eLeader means making the loud statements that demonstrate to your workforce, your senior managers, your shareholders, and the public that you are ready to lead the change effort. It's a very personal commitment. Ask yourself if you are ready to do what you say—if you are ready not only to speak the creed but also to do the deed.

- *To delegate office space—even yours—according to need, not title?*
- *To make the tough decisions—about cannibalizing products, shifting directions, investing in the future—and then talk face to face with employees about these decisions?*
- *To fire top managers who make their numbers but reinforce behaviors of the past?*
- *To reward and recognize managers who break the rules, but are also leading you into the future?*
- *To slaughter your company's sacred cows, even if they are things like a favored project, a perk you enjoy, or a conventional way of doing business?*
- *To look vulnerable—to be in meetings with employees where you don't know all the answers—and to admit your own mistakes?*
- *To answer any question your workers offer?*
- *To say things out loud that your workforce does not want to hear?*
- *To sit down and have lunch with your employees?*
- *To hold the senior leadership team accountable to predetermine behaviors essential for changing the organization?*
- *To share company ownership and profits with all employees, not just the senior leadership team?*

6

Communicate Irreverently

You communicate with your employees face to face, in speeches and meetings. You communicate with them through printed materials, including memos, newsletters, internal magazines, and notes on the bulletin board. And increasingly, you communicate with them via technology: voice mail, email, videoconferences, intranets, and the like.

But you also communicate with your employees through the way you configure your desks, the music in your elevator—even the music playing on the phone when callers are put on hold.

As you redesign employee communications to support your company's transition to the New Economy, you must grasp this critical concept: You are talking to your workforce all the time, and not just through the official communication vehicles. Everything from office space design to employee compensation sends messages. It's all communications.

And all communication, whether intended or not, encourages behavior by sending an implicit or explicit message.

At every juncture, with every communication vehicle, an eLeader must stop and think: What is our new strategic direction? What behaviors are necessary to support that strategic direction? And how does this communication reinforce those behaviors?

It is like creating a road map. The corporate strategies drive you to the appropriate behaviors, which in turn are signaled by the right communication vehicles. Each vehicle has to be tested against the road map.

You already have sketched out your company's road map. You have a strategy in place and have pinpointed behaviors that support that strategy.

You have examined the implicit and explicit rules at your organization to determine whether they support the new work environment you're building. You have made a loud statement that breaks some of those unwanted implicit rules and demonstrates that change is on the way.

Now you must conduct a similar inventory of your communication tools and analyze the behaviors they reinforce—particularly through implicit messages.

What messages are sent and what behavior is reinforced through the layout and size of offices? By a two-page dress code—in an era where we are encouraging independent thought and personal accountability? By the format and location of staff meetings? What about your pay scale—how does it convey your company's feelings about its employees?

As you move forward into the New Economy, it's imperative that all these messages are integrated and work together to facilitate change. As you find implicit messages that don't fit your change initiative—messages that encourage behaviors of the past—get rid of them. Break the old rules.

You must approach employee communications with a new irreverence in the spirit of your loud statement of change.

Your overall goal is to improve your business position by creating an environment of speed, agility, creativity, and flexibility. Make sure your ongoing employee communications work toward that goal by breaking with the past, slaughtering sacred cows, and continually reinforcing your loud statement of change.

Organic's Story:
Turning Conventional Wisdom on Its Head

Started in a San Francisco apartment several years ago, Organic is an Internet professional services company that has grown to encompass offices from London to São Paulo to Chicago.

Like many fast-growing Internet companies, Organic depends on the collaboration between pragmatic baby boomers (who provide business and management experience) and Generation X and Y staffers (who provide technical expertise and creative energy).

When the leaders of Organic's Manhattan office began thinking about a community-building event for its three hundred staffers, "We were really taken with the fact that so many of us spent so much time explaining to people what we did at work," says Kate Swann, vice-president and managing director of the New York office. "And many of those people were our families."

But because so many Organic workers are young and single, they weren't explaining their jobs to their kids, or even their spouses. They were talking to their parents.

That led Organic to sponsor a "Bring Your Parents to Work Day" in November 1999.

"We are a company that is all about innovations. In that spirit, we decided to turn the old 'Bring Your Kids to Work Day' concept on its head," Swann says. "And it was something that absolutely made sense to people as we started to talk about it.

"It wasn't just the youth of our workforce, but also the industry that we are in—and the amount of change we deal with on a day-to-day basis. This event could be a way to challenge ourselves to explain to our families, and to ourselves, what we do here and why."

Sending out invitations with only three weeks' notice, Organic management wasn't quite sure what to expect. They were stunned when 125 parents—and grandparents—showed up, flying in from places as far away as Taiwan, Seattle, and Los Angeles.

Everyone assembled in the morning for doughnuts and coffee. "We went around the room and asked each parent, 'What do you think your child does?'" says Swann, thirty-seven, who invited her own mother-in-law. Replied one mother of a systems analyst, "When we ask her what she does, she talks to us for twenty minutes. And we still don't know what she does. But whatever it is, we're proud of her."

The group was shown a short video introducing Organic, with a tongue-in-cheek approach to the insider jargon and acronyms of the high-tech world. Starring Organic's creative director—playing "Dr. Vrml" in a campy Mr. Wizard-style format—the video included mock interviews with "concerned parents" discussing their children.

"Ever since she enrolled in a course called Interactive Design, we haven't understood a thing out of her mouth," said one "parent." "What is an information architect? Why am I paying for her student loans while she's got stock options?"

After the lighthearted introduction, the visitors were treated to a three-hour tour of the Organic lifestyle. The organizers gave everyone a map of speaking stations where they could see Organic work in progress, ask questions, and hear short presentations.

"Parents were asking questions that brought the work we were doing into a completely new context," Swann says. "I mean, these were the customers of our clients we had a chance to talk to, and explain things to."

Finally, everyone was treated to the standard Organic meeting menu: pizza.

"It was a very energizing experience. The perspective on what we take for granted about our work style was incredibly valuable," Swann says.

Coverage on CNN and in both the local New York newspapers and the high-tech press didn't hurt, either.

The event was so unexpectedly successful that Organic repeated it in other offices and has planned a global event, with every Organic office hosting a Parents Day on the same date.

"Employees appreciated the company understanding their perspective; it added to their sense of Organic as a place where they can create value," Swann says.

"But it also challenged us to talk about what we do in a different way than we normally do. That was a terrific exercise as well."

Open the Toolbox

As Organic's story demonstrates, communicating effectively with employees requires creativity, planning, and sensitivity—and sometimes a little bit of luck. But it is not brain surgery. Still, most companies don't do it well.

They spend thousands and thousands of dollars on consultants, management meetings, employee surveys, customer research—and create a plan for change. But they neglect to follow up their initiative with consistent, coordinated communications with the people who ultimately must execute that plan: their employees.

Or perhaps the company begins the change effort, gets everyone pumped up, and then returns to the same staid, predictable employee communications vehicles to promote the change message.

Imagine attending a dynamic, inspiring meeting that features provocative Q&A sessions, funny or touching video messages, and eye-opening games. Lots of emotion and commitment on display.

What a letdown it would be to arrive back at the office and

find the old black-and-white employee newsletter sitting on your desk.

That is not to say that a newsletter or magazine can't be a terrific vehicle to communicate change. In fact, it's wise to remember that simply being clever or using high-tech tools on their own doesn't necessarily reinforce the right behavior. A town-hall meeting may look like a loud statement of change but if it's not planned specifically to reinforce the right behaviors, it will be a feel-good meeting without a strategic purpose.

Everything you use to communicate should be measured against your strategic objectives and reflect the behaviors you want to encourage within your organization—those behaviors required to implement strategy effectively.

With that in mind, open the toolbox and use everything you can think of to communicate change to your employees:

- The work environment—in its broadest sense
- People—at all levels of your organization
- Meetings, formal and informal
- Compensation
- Simple things
- High-tech tools
- Games and contests
- Formal messages

Use all these tools, and use them in unexpected ways.

Scient Corp. uses its technology and its people to communicate with its employees. It's created more than twenty "neighborhoods" where employees from across the company who share similar work-related obsessions—like a particular programming language or software—can form a group and with monetary support from the company, advance innovation in the company as they are bonding as individuals. Scient's employees, who tend to be isolated in their job tasks, feel part of a larger community and the company reinforces its commitment to innovation.

Save the Environment

At Organic's New York office, you get the message as soon as you walk in the door and see pool and foosball tables, videogames, and gathering spots on each floor. This environment has been set up so employees can have fun and be creative.

"We try things to encourage people just to come together," Kate Swann says.

Organic also has done what a growing number of companies are doing: Rather than allocate precious window space to top executives, the company has kept the windows clear of offices, so that everyone can share the natural light and views of Manhattan. It's a physical manifestation of Organic's democratic approach.

Everything about your organization's work environment sends a message to employees as well as clients, investors, and visitors. As you are reassessing your employee communications, take a look at how those environmental messages match up with your desired behaviors.

Susan Silk, president of MSI Strategic Communications, is an eLeader who thought about what behaviors she wanted to foster in her employees and used the work environment to help accomplish that goal.

MSI is a fourteen-person firm called in to troubleshoot its clients' communications problems. Because of its size, and because of the creative and fast-paced nature of its work, MSI needed to promote "a high level of energy, a lot of assertive behavior, and a sense of communal learning as fast as we can," Silk says.

Because most of its client projects involve external communications, MSI is "part of the news environment," Silk says. To reflect that, Silk designed the office to resemble a traditional newsroom: A leader sits in the center with his team members seated around him in a ring. There are no private offices, and virtually no privacy. "People can see each other, hear each other, talk to each other, and overhear each other. The explosion of information instantly turns into common knowledge," Silk says.

Of course, the newsroom layout also was fun. "The last thing I wanted was for the outside world to confuse us with an insurance company—or for my employees to think they were working in an insurance company," Silk says. "This is a creative business. I need people to feel good enough and happy enough that they take leaps, that they're willing to go for it."

Silk is the first to admit that it's not the perfect environment for everyone. Even though she's created quiet corners people can use when they need to write and think to themselves, MSI's office is a place full of hubbub and energy.

But it has yielded the desired results. Client satisfaction is high. External studies have demonstrated to her that productivity is extremely high compared to competitors, such as DDB Needham and Leo Burnett Co., with strong results in such measurements as employee hours versus overhead.

"The environment has reinforced the skills we need," Silk says. "We move fast. It's a very collaborative environment. If we are headed down a wrong road, everyone hears it and jumps in, and we can adjust accordingly."

MSI has succeeded so well that it needs more room. The company is preparing to move and double its office space. This time, Silk's idea is to create an unstructured environment with furniture on wheels, where virtual teams can assemble when and for as long as necessary. "Pods" will have room for three people. "If two people are working together on a project for two weeks, they can sit right next to each other for those two weeks. They won't need scheduled meetings or memos to communicate," she says. "Then two weeks later, those people can move on to the next project and their next officemates."

MSI's new space also will have two private offices for its two vice-presidents. Silk has allowed that for several reasons: First, the seven-year-old organization has matured to the point where the leaders don't need to micromanage. Second, she believes that giving junior employees distance from their manager "will cause them to take more responsibility." Again, she is using the physical design of her office space to promote certain behaviors.

The master of using physical space to reflect his organizational philosophy may be Carl Russo. When Carl created and ran his own high-tech company, Cerent, he wanted to create an egalitarian environment that encouraged maximum creativity.

All the conference rooms and other public spaces that required walls were located in the center of the building, so that the entire outside of the building was glass. And how close you sat to the windows, Russo says, "was inversely proportional to your title."

Every Cerent employee had a low-walled, eight-foot-by-eight-foot cube. (Because Carl was a manager, he allowed himself the standard cube and also an adjoining cube.)

"It took a little while to help people through this," Russo says. The low walls created a louder, more interactive atmosphere that engineers initially objected to, but they opted for headphones if they needed privacy.

The corners of the Cerent building were not consumed by executive offices. Instead, each corner was decorated around a theme—the beach, the sixties—and was designed as a space where employees could interact. Russo paid local restaurants to bring in food and drink for breakfast, lunch, and dinner. And the amazing thing, he says, is that "people congregated there."

You might not be able to be quite so creative. But remember that every detail about how your office space is designed sends a message about how you want your employees to approach their jobs:

- Office location: Downtown, suburbs, off the highway? New building, old building?
- Colors on the walls and floor: Bright or subdued?

- Configuration of individual offices: Are there doors and windows (and who has them)? High walls or low walls? Big offices or small?
- Lobby and public spaces: Formal (marble, mahogany, traditional tables and chairs) or informal (glass, exposed brick/wires/ducts)?
- Art: Modern and funky? Traditional?
- Furniture: Functional or comfortable?

Nextera worked with the information technology department of one large company where low morale, high attrition, and a lack of teamwork were big issues. After focus groups with employees, we toured the office space: It was a place without windows, without space to stretch or think or gather together. It was a place full of cubes and lists of rules. It was clear that employees found it difficult to work there.

We suggested that the company have a "Tear Down the Walls Day," where the employees could rearrange the walls in order to make the space more comfortable, more collaborative, and more fun. We suggested that the workers decide how to use the office's one big empty space. They could choose the functionality themselves, and then decorate it.

Unfortunately, the company management rejected the recommendation, saying they had to follow the rules of the building. Ultimately, this company was willing to risk high employee turnover in a very competitive market simply to follow the rules.

In this tight job market, smart companies are learning how to use the office environment to keep valued employees productive and motivated. But a work environment is not merely physical space.

As senior vice-president of human resources, Mark Stavish oversees the people side of what America Online calls its Value Added Equation. His goal, he says, "is to build a work environment that's simple and easy to navigate. As people's personal lives blend closer and closer to their business lives, being able to provide the extra amenities and services that make their lives a little easier is important."

At AOL headquarters, that means a place to drop off and pick up dry cleaning. It means a small store on the premises where employees can buy sundries. It means a free concierge service to help arrange travel plans or a child's birthday party. It means extended hours at the company cafeteria so employees working late can get a meal to take home if necessary.

The relatively small amount AOL pays to have these services available, Stavish says, is worth it because "we know that providing these services takes a little complexity out of our employees' lives. And that complexity would take time away from what they really want to do, which hopefully are their jobs here."

As you pinpoint the behaviors you want from your employees, assess how your current environment does or does not support those behaviors. Many companies have experimented with "virtual" mobile offices, desks on wheels, creative "thought rooms," and other unusual workspace ideas. Others have installed such amenities as daycare centers and fitness rooms.

Consider how you might change your current environment to better reflect the company you want to be—and attract and retain the best and brightest employees.

F2F: Take It to the People

If your work environment is the biggest and most flexible tool you have to communicate with your employees, people probably are the most effective tool. In a far-flung world of faxes, email, and voice mail, face-to-face communication is more important than ever.

There's a role for formal communications—with a capital C—and there is a role for the communication that happens on a day-to-day basis in the hall or in meetings. Smart companies can use their top 20% performers as ambassadors of change in those day-to-day communications.

Among any company's top 20% are natural leaders who are eager for change, who embrace the change message and instinctively begin modeling the new behaviors. Formalize the role of those people by creating a team of Change Champions: high-performance individuals who are responsible for reinforcing desired behaviors, identifying new barriers to change, and recognizing other employees or teams of employees who have success stories to tell.

When searching for Change Champions, look for people who:

- Others rely on and go to for information
- Are well respected by everyone—peers, subordinates and bosses alike

- Are flexible and willing to break the rules to achieve business results
- Instinctively respect other people
- Are persistent and positive even in uncertain situations
- Are enthused about the learning opportunities during the change process

A Change Champion team will be an invaluable way to reach into the corners of your organization with your change message.

They weren't called Change Champions, but following CCH's two-hour live videoconference to launch its change effort, we created a similar team of change agents: a squad of sixty individuals located throughout the company and identified by large "Just Ask Me" buttons. The team's mission was to answer employee questions and address concerns about the reengineering process.

Just Ask Me leaders had been trained to help fellow employees through the change process—first by letting the individual vent any hostility, resistance or fear of change, then by answering the question.

In follow-up research, we found that 40% of CCH employees had consulted a Just Ask Me team member. We knew that every opportunity to answer a question was also an opportunity to reinforce new behaviors, face to face.

CCH relied on a lot of top 20% performers to bolster its change communications program. But sometimes companies can recruit members of the middle 60% to communicate during times of upheaval.

In the mid-nineties, GATX Terminals, a leading provider

of bulk liquid storage and distribution, was in trouble. Conditions in the oil industry were creating huge overcapacity problems and earnings were dropping dramatically. Workers at the company's ten terminals were worried about their jobs, about their facilities being sold, and about the plans of a recently installed GATX management team. That team had devised a new corporate strategy, but found it difficult to get the message out beyond corporate headquarters.

"Supervisors in the field would call me and say, 'What do I say to my people? They're screaming at me. What am I going to tell them? I don't know how to talk to them,'" remembers Teri Schram, then the company's head of internal communications.

Schram broke the rules by offering key communicator training for the men who ran the terminals—"hard hat–type guys who had been in the business for thirty years," she says. In half-day sessions at each terminal, these supervisors got an eye-opening experience. Role-playing exercises helped these men figure out what their workers were actually saying as they complained about the company. They also became aware of how their pat corporate responses sounded to a truly concerned questioner.

Trainees were taught to let concerned people vent their emotions, to listen for the real message behind the anger, and then to avoid management-speak as they answered questions honestly.

After one training session, an older supervisor came up to Schram and said he was ashamed to admit how he had talked to his employees over the years; it was now clear to him what kinds of off-putting messages he had sent as he thought he was doing the right thing. He had tried to protect people by not admitting there were problems, and by putting a positive spin on everything.

As you use people as your surrogates in the field, don't forget your senior leadership team.

When DSM Desotech decided that despite its market leadership and sales growth, it needed to position itself for future challenges, the company's management style became a primary target. Everyone relied on CEO Ken Lawson for decisions and answers. In the future, the company knew it needed to push accountability and responsibility down through the organization.

The centerpiece of the company's "Do What's Best for the Business" initiative was an effort to change employee behavior. But before they announced the initiative, DSM Desotech's senior leadership team spent more than nine months in training, learning and practicing the new behavior so that they could model it for the rest of the organization.

In this key communicator training, Desotech's leaders learned what they needed to communicate the company's new push for accountability. They listed the kinds of behaviors the company needed to promote. They engaged in role-playing sessions to learn how to talk to employees in a way that reinforced those behaviors. In mock Q&A sessions, they took turns answering anticipated questions.

When the senior team was ready, the initiative was announced, a kickoff meeting was held, and then Lawson made sure that every single Desotech employee went through culture change classes to get hands-on exposure to the new desired behaviors.

The company followed up the training by creating a three-part video called "Whatever Happened to John Q. Culture?" Starring the senior leaders, the mock radio mystery show made fun of the old behaviors Desotech was trying to excise.

Telling people to act differently in a meeting or memo is no guarantee that they will do anything differently. Push the desired behaviors down through your organization by using everyone from your senior leadership team to floor supervisors—and make sure they have the consistent learning and coaching they need to do the job.

Get It on the Grapevine

Just as a company has both official and unofficial communications vehicles, an organization can use people both as official communicators—and as unofficial reporters.

Every organization has a grapevine made up of people who are trusted by others as reliable sources of information. Sometimes they are really reliable, and sometimes not—but in either case, they are hooked in and they have credibility with their fellow workers.

The grapevine is invaluable. First, these people are able to tell you what the workforce is really thinking from a grassroots perspective. They love to tell you; they are proud to know what they know. But what they love even more is to get news and to spread it as far and fast as possible.

One CEO puts it this way: "I always thought the best way to communicate something to the company was to mention it to the guy next to me in the men's room. Before I knew it, the news would be everywhere."

But if you're smart, you can use these people in more strategic ways. After all, they are your company's unofficial thought leaders.

When I worked as a corporate communicator, I got to know these people and would use them when I needed to get a story out. If I had something to announce, I'd call all these people. The news eventually would come out in newsletters, memos, or email, but the grapevine heard it first.

Or I would sit down with these people and listen to their comments and concerns and try to focus them in the direction of change. I could get a handle on what people really were thinking. And if I was persuasive, they then could be the company's unofficial evangelists for change.

In one story illustrating the value of the grapevine, a CEO had been sent an email by someone in the workforce. The employee challenged a human resources benefit that he didn't like. Unfortunately, it happened to be a benefit program that the CEO personally had toiled over for several months in an attempt to be fair to everyone.

When the CEO opened the critical email, his feelings were hurt: He'd spent six months on this initiative and instead of getting thanked, he'd been slammed. So he did a very human thing: He sent a return email that blasted the employee's opinion.

It didn't take long for him to realize that he'd made a mistake. But he couldn't retrieve the email; the damage was done. I encouraged him to break the rules and tell the truth.

If he thought he'd handled the situation badly, he should own up to it—and apologize.

He did. He wrote the employee an email explaining how hard he'd worked on that benefits plan, how much he'd wanted to be fair, and how his feelings were wounded by the criticism. He apologized.

As the CEO was sending out the apologetic email, his communications person called the grapevine to tell them what he was doing. And that email, and the story behind it, went around the world. Everyone remembered what an honest guy the CEO was. The grapevine did its job.

Meet New Expectations

Employees dread meetings. But if you have delivered your loud statement of change through a big, dramatic meeting, you know how effective and inspirational these gatherings can be.

The best way to communicate the change message accurately to your employees is to have everyone share that big event—by getting everyone in one room or by hooking them up to a videoconference. CCH actually did that when it was making its loud statement of change: Every out-of-town employee was connected to the meeting either by video or by phone line, and each person had a chance to ask questions.

But CCH had a relatively manageable number of employees, in relatively few locations. For companies with many employees in many offices, such a one-time event may be impossible to coordinate.

For those companies, an option may be a "meeting in a

box": a toolkit that allows managers to recreate the big event experience back home, with their own department or division. A manager can play a videotape with highlights of the big meeting, and perhaps follow the same meeting format to lead discussions and contests. A few pages of talking points can help the local managers accurately send the message of change throughout the organization.

ABN AMRO NA, the North American arm of the Dutch banking giant, had developed a new strategic plan. The company had shared the plan with all of its senior leaders, but that barely scratched the surface; Kim Woods, director of internal communications, wanted to reach as many of the company's eighteen thousand employees as possible. Since those employees work in hundreds of individual banks and financial services offices, the only viable alternative was to let local managers run their own smaller meetings.

The meeting in a box, Woods says, "gave managers everything they needed to conduct the presentation": a PowerPoint presentation, a videotape, and even cue cards for a speech. The kit also contained a set of small laminated cards, one for each employee. The cards offered a snapshot of the company, listing the company's corporate values, management principles, goals and strategy, and a brief organizational breakdown. Since it reformulated its strategy in 1999, ABN AMRO has sent out more than fourteen hundred meeting kits.

"With this program, we shared more information about this company, what we do and what our goals are than has ever been shared with employees before," Woods says.

Another option is to follow a big event with a series of town hall meetings, where smaller groups of employees can have a chance to ask questions of senior managers and get more detailed answers.

Once these big, powerful meetings raise employee expectations about how the company is changing, your challenge is to make every face-to-face meeting with employees as compelling and engaging as possible—even the small ones.

DSM Desotech has kept its change effort going with monthly "Sunrise Symposiums," which start at 7:00 A.M. Over a continental breakfast, employees get the company's latest financial news, hear updates on problem areas, share success stories, and obtain information on topics from human resources benefits to workplace safety.

"We have an opportunity to share the same story with everyone," says chairman Ken Lawson.

Unusual meeting times are one attention-getting technique; other companies hold employee meetings in unusual locations, like the stairwell of the headquarters building, to avoid the same old boring framework.

Dave Tolmie, CEO of yesmail.com, chooses to stand on a table in the middle of the office to conduct his monthly employee meetings. "Short of absolutely the most confidential information, everybody knows exactly what's going on," Tolmie says. "A lot of times it's information they maybe shouldn't have, but they get it anyway."

Tolmie also has informal meetings with his workers—to get to know everyone, answer questions, and keep the staff up to date. Under a scheme he calls "Dining with Dave," he regularly takes his employees to lunch, five or six at a time.

"I think communication is really important—lots of it," he says. "We're growing really fast, and there's a lot going on. We need to be on the same page."

Brad Keywell, CEO of Starbelly.com, has a similar program he calls "Star Buddies." The program randomly selects groups of five employees from different parts of the company. Starbelly pays them to go out to lunch together every three weeks.

"The receptionist may be buddies with our head of technology, or the head of marketing with a programmer," Keywell says. "We all learn from each other what we're doing. We all learn something new."

But recognizing that to some degree, everyone dreads meetings, Keywell has one other firm and fast rule: No meeting can last more than thirty minutes.

For companies seeking speed and agility, that may be the best message of all to send.

Check Your Pay Plans

We're human. We can't help it: We judge ourselves, our bosses, and our employer by the way we are paid.

Compensation philosophy always will be one of the important ways an organization communicates with its employees. It's essential that your compensation encourage and reward the right employee behaviors.

Put your money where your mouth is: If you can, tie your bonuses, promotions, and raises directly to new desired behaviors. Create a bonus program for nonmanagers—put some percentage of payroll into a fund used to reward specific employee contributions on a periodic basis.

One global company wanted to stress to managers the importance of valuing people. Its solution was to use employee surveys to rate their engagement with their jobs—and then to connect managers' promotions to their success in getting employees engaged.

A second company decided to withhold its managers' bonuses until they turned in evaluations of their employees; the return rate on completed evaluations went up 30 percent in two years.

A third company didn't pay its employees until they entered their project learnings into a companywide database.

These are short-term uses of compensation to reinforce the importance of new behaviors. You may need to consider long-term shifts in your compensation systems and institute specialized pay structures, particularly if you are creating an eBusiness venture or subsidiary.

The Internet has changed the way we view pay; compensating employees at an eBusiness is no more like traditional pay than an Internet start-up's structure is like that of a mature Fortune 500 company. To encourage the right risk-taking, fast-moving behaviors, an eBusiness needs to create a similarly aggressive pay plan.

In these new ePay structures, providing employees with equity in the new venture has become critical in attracting and retaining the best talent. It's also a motivation to high performance. That equity can take the form of:

- Options for the parent company's stock
- Parent company stock options based on the internal eVenture's performance
- Phantom stock options
- Tracking stock options
- Options for the subsidiary's stock
- A leveraged coinvestment

No matter what your company's specific challenge, remember that the best and brightest employees you need to make your transition into the New Economy—particularly those members of Generations X and Y—will not be satisfied with "one size fits all" compensation plans. These coveted workers want to be rewarded as individuals, for their individual performance, in a manner appropriate for the risk they are taking working for you.

Try a Simple Thing

Despite all the talk of stock options and equity in the headlines today, I do not believe most top 20% employees are motivated primarily by money. It may be a lure if they are unhappy and want to leave a job. Instead, keep them happy not just with financial rewards, but also with simple expressions of appreciation.

Lisa White of pointpathbank.com sends restaurant gift certificates to her employees' spouses to show how much she appreciates the family time they sacrifice for their jobs. Scient Corp. gives new parents an engraved silver baby spoon from Tiffany & Company to celebrate.

Kim Woods of ABN AMRO NA endorses the "simple things—like little note cards, like if someone stayed late, or worked extra hard on a special project. It's kind of like going back to the basics and showing your appreciation in a way that a lot of people don't take time to do anymore: Stop for a second, compliment someone on a job well done, recognize them and go back.

"Some of those nonmonetary rewards are getting lost a lot of times now because we're so busy. We're trying to bring back that feeling where people felt like they were part of a family or a community. We don't want the personal interaction of work to get lost as we move forward and transform ourselves into an eBusiness."

You can get irreverent with the simple things as well. Brad Keywell has a masseuse come in three times a week to ease the stress of Starbelly's employees. In addition, the company has a yoga instructor come in twice a week, and twice a month hosts introspective "drum circles."

Even if only a few people participate, all of your employees will think it's a great idea—and that it reflects the way your company feels about its employees.

"These are all ways to communicate better," Keywell says. It couldn't be simpler.

Try Out High-Tech Helpers

There's a time for high touch, and a time for high tech.

There is no doubt that technology very rapidly has expanded the ways companies can communicate with their employees—and made those communications dramatically more timely and lively.

Most companies now have email and voice mail functions that can be used to reach employees quickly and personally. Many also have intranets and websites for internal use.

As you would expect, technology giant 3Com does all these things. But even a high-tech provider can figure out something new that really works well.

3Com schedules regular CEO forums with its employees. A recent forum followed the release of the company's quarterly results. It was a two-way live broadcast that linked the company's CEO in California; its employees, located around the world; and the COO and a group of product managers who were in New York for an important trade show.

3Com had rented a brownstone house in downtown New York, just down the street from the conference center. Technological wizards turned this 110-year-old house into a "digital house" showcasing the products and technologies 3Com also had been demonstrating at the trade show. The press, clients, and investment analysts were invited along.

A satellite broadcast originated from the house's third floor. The CEO spoke first from the Santa Clara headquarters, then turned the show over to the COO in the New York house, who introduced a prerecorded house tour. Following that was a taped report of happenings on the trade show floor. Then product managers hosted a live demonstration of the new tools on display at the house and participated in a Q&A session.

Through the satellite broadcast or downloads, 3Com employees could watch the session from their locations anywhere in the world. They could ask a question by typing it into their desktop computer. And if they missed it, the whole meeting was then posted onto the company's 3Community intranet.

3Com is going through a lot of change, and employee communications tools like these are a critical part of corporate strategy. "We are going through a period of major transition," says Mark Levine, director of employee communications. "We are trying to help people come along with that change and help them understand it. And these sorts of messages are most powerful when they come from our leadership—as they did in this recent forum."

Similarly, catalogue retailer J. Crew, which is conducting a companywide reengineering of technology and systems, wants to keep all employees invested in the change effort. The company has created an internal website where all the information about the effort—from meeting minutes to project plans to executive biographies—is available to all employees all the time.

Banking giant ABN AMRO NA traditionally relied on a print newsletter and magazine for much of its employee communications. But the company just hit the desktop computers of fifteen thousand of its North American employees with a new enterprise information portal.

The new portal, called Currency, streamlines the way employees receive information and company news and they way they access their software applications. The portal offers a toolbox with company phone and location directories, templates for business correspondence and presentations, plus national phone directories. Through the portal, employees can access human resources functions and change their address on paychecks and fill out a new W-4 form for tax withholding.

In addition, "My Currency Page" has a mechanism for the company to send a news flash across the employee's computer screen. "It's very quick, even faster than email," says Kim Woods, internal communications director.

ABN AMRO soon will publish its weekly employee newsletter on the portal and will begin phasing out other print publications. For consideration down the road: sections of the portal customized for different business functions (investment banking, consumer banking, and so forth); chat rooms; and two-way survey and feedback tools.

At Sibson, we've used a couple of high-tech tools to keep our employees posted on hot news, right away. President Roger Brossy, for instance, ran video messages and interviews on Sibson's intranet.

And last year we allowed all of our employees to eavesdrop on one of our partners' meetings: The company took audio excerpts from the meeting, along with postmeeting comments from Brossy, edited them into a single tape, and posted that onto the intranet. Just hours after the meeting ended, everyone at the company received an email link to the audio broadcast.

"Most of the tape was live. It wasn't scripted. And it wasn't just me. It was in the moment, a clip of all eleven of us talking and reacting," Brossy says. "It was available within hours of the meeting's end—so there was none of that typical waiting to see whether black smoke or white smoke was rising from the meeting room. It was right there for everyone to listen to."

High-tech tools are a great way to make your company communications faster and very democratic.

Play a Game

As great as technology is, sometimes a low-tech idea—a game or contest—can send the right message to employees and engage their attention as well.

Following a big meeting kicking off a change program, the North American division of a global company created a program challenging its leaders to implement concrete solutions to encourage new behaviors and overcome cultural barriers. Each month, managers could submit their teams' initiatives to be judged and awarded points based on their scope and effectiveness.

The submissions were featured in a new newsletter that objectively reported the results each month and offered vivid descriptions to serve as models of new, desired behaviors. An intranet site included electronic submission forms and a running tally of each team's points.

The contest was fun, and it worked. Employees everywhere began streamlining processes and eliminating unproductive work. One group saved hundreds of thousands of dollars in production costs. Another team took the push for risk-taking seriously and made a $13 million gamble that paid big dividends.

CCH had invested $1 million to renovate a critical print fulfillment center. But the investment seemingly had been wasted. Despite new state-of-the-art equipment, only half of all orders were being shipped within three days.

The problem was that the plant was being run as it always had been run—from the top down. Workers had no authority and no accountability. Consequently, the physical renovation was not enough to improve productivity.

CCH worked to improve morale at the plant, and then introduced a goal for the facility workforce: Deliver perfect products on time. To accomplish the goal, employees were asked to work on three behaviors: to focus on customers, accept personal responsibility, and communicate openly and honestly. Meeting together, the workers came up with a tagline for their effort: "Perfect Products on Time."

To encourage employees to adopt those three behaviors, the staff created three games.

In "Catch a Behavior," employees nominated fellow workers who were "caught" exhibiting one of the new behaviors. "Perfect Attendance Rules" rewarded workers who arrived on time every day and scheduled personal days in advance. And the big one, "Get Those Orders Out the Door," required plant employees to ship 85 percent of all orders within three days for three consecutive months.

When the three months were over and 90 percent of orders had been shipped within three days, CCH threw a huge party for everyone at the center. The message had been received, loudly and clearly.

Send the Write Message

In this new world of irreverent communications, there still is an important role for formal Employee Communications—with a capital C. These are valuable tools to tell stories that demonstrate exactly what you mean by new behaviors.

The staple of employee communications is the written word. Don't take any of those words for granted: Use every opportunity to model, encourage, and demonstrate strategy-driven behaviors through written communications with your employees.

Organizations tend to pay close attention to the big, dramatic statements of change and make sure those are "on message." Then they will defeat themselves by letting tradition, bureaucracy, and other "old" behavior creep back into everyday memos and letters. Make sure every memo buttresses the change effort in its tone and format.

Deliver your message effectively to the right audience, check for cultural and political sensitivities, and continually reinforce new behaviors.

As long as you are taking dramatic steps to deliver a new message of change, make sure people are paying attention by creating new, vibrant communications tools. It's probably time to rename, redesign, or ditch your old employee newsletter and internal magazine. Just seeing the same old format arrive on their desks may make workers tune out immediately.

Some companies opt to turn their stories into video newsmagazines, a la ABC-TV's *20/20*.

When Nextera conducted employee focus groups for Ernst

& Young's Lake Michigan region in late 1998, we found that employees felt the company valued its clients much more than it valued its staff. In addition, several corporate practices had become annoying to employees and clearly were getting in the way of change.

So before E&Y launched its yearlong "People Add Value" campaign, it sent a videotape to each employee's home. Arriving near New Year's Day 1999, the videotape—tagged "E&Y Action News"—was a mock investigative news program.

The host, a former TV news reporter, had been given the mission of uncovering the reasons behind E&Y's recent slew of professional awards. A camera crew filmed him in the offices of the region's three top leaders. With tongues firmly in cheek, each executive attributed the E&Y success to a different cultural barrier that had been driving employees crazy.

One executive took aim at the company's policy of "hoteling"—having employees share office space. Another made fun of the prevalence of alphabet acronyms. And the third picked on what had become a Byzantine organizational structure.

Following the farce, the reporter conducted serious interviews with E&Y employees who were demonstrating the desired behaviors of collegiality, innovation, and accountability—the behaviors really behind E&Y's industry awards. Those reports were followed by a wrap-up message from the region's managing partner, thanking everyone for their hard work and promising an improved work environment through the "People Add Value" campaign.

Despite everyone's interest in technology, there may be

occasions when a plain old printed newsletter will be the most cost-effective and viable way to get out the company news. And it doesn't have to be boring.

As GATX Terminals was instituting a new corporate strategy to cope with difficult market conditions, it needed to find a way to encourage new behavior among the workers in the company's ten terminals. GATX wanted to encourage people to be more flexible, to think differently about the business, to take risks, and to be more creative.

But this was a company where "there had been no communications before, ever," Teri Schram says. "Unless you had something big and definitive to say, you didn't tell anybody anything." That was especially true of the workers in the field, who had minimal contact with headquarters and with employees at other terminals.

That meant no one knew who the best workers were, or what other terminals were doing. There was no sharing of best practices.

What Schram did was to create a campaign called "Not The Same Old." Volunteers—largely the office staff at each terminal—were commissioned as "reporters" and sent out to find story leads: creative new business efforts, solutions to common problems, and other news. The stories were written back at headquarters by a professional journalist and turned into a newsletter that everyone read, used, and loved.

Schram's "Not The Same Old" newsletter was successful in large part because of its honesty. If you are trying to create an environment of innovation, the stories in your newsletter—or your meetings, or anywhere else—can't just give the results. They have to tell the process of getting to the results. That includes the mistakes, the tries, the lucky accidents.

Most formal communications tools in companies today are merely propaganda, and employees treat them that way. As you start telling stories of your change effort, don't change the stories to follow the old implicit communication rules. Don't homogenize the stories. People don't know it, but they guard the old rules.

Your job as eLeader has to be to monitor your company's storytelling to make sure it's really reinforcing the right behaviors.

Addressing the Middle

All of these employee communications tools will help you talk to the key subsets of your workforce.

By bringing your actions and words into alignment, these communications will increase your credibility with the important Generation X and Y staffers.

By reinforcing the loud statement of change, you will let your top 20% performers know that they should hang in there during the change effort—that you are actively working to take care of the cultural barriers that have made their jobs more difficult.

But there is no doubt that these messages are primarily geared toward the middle 60% of your workforce, that movable middle. Whether it's a contest, an interactive forum, or a sharpened newsletter, these programs and tools are designed to engage them in the change process—to show them why change is happening and why it's important, and to reinforce the right behaviors for them.

The next step in the eLeader's journey is creating heroes—a step that will further engage the middle 60% by giving them real-life examples upon which to model their behavior.

CHECKLIST FOR CREATING
CULTURALLY SENSITIVE COMMUNICATIONS

The following list is designed to help eLeaders communicate more effectively around the world. The questions below will help you write and edit text in a manner that is clear and avoids cultural sensitivities.

❑ *Have you written your message as concisely and simply as possible? Are the sentences in simple English? Have you inserted bullets or numbered steps to make it organized and easy to follow?*

❑ *If you refer to times, places, and dates, have you inserted the time zone? Have you used the format dd/mm/yy?*

❑ *Have you avoided the use of colloquialisms, metaphors, jargon, and local expressions? Have you defined any new acronyms or technical terms?*

❑ *If you provide a telephone/fax contact number, is it accessible to all who need to use it? (For instance, toll-free 800 numbers do not work outside of North America.)*

❑ *When your message is targeted to a particular audience,*

have you made that distinction clear in the subject line, title, and/or in the first few sentences of the body?

❑ Have you proofread or spell-checked your document using the form of English your audience uses?

❑ Have you chosen the appropriate author/deliverer for the message? Would your message have greater impact if it came from a different source?

❑ If the audience is unfamiliar with the author, has the author's full name and role been included somewhere in the message?

❑ When you are unsure about the potential cultural and/or political sensitivities of your message, have you found someone to review your draft and give you open and honest feedback?

Note: Checklist created by Nextera's Bronwyn Poole and Caroline Chubb.

CHECKLIST FOR ALIGNMENT WITH DESIRED STRATEGY, CULTURE, AND BEHAVIORS

This list is designed to help you write and edit text in alignment with your firm's desired strategy, culture, and behaviors.

STRATEGY

❑ Does your message identify why change is necessary and make a strong "business case for change"? Is the information clearly connected to the strategic imperatives of your firm?

❑ If your message is about customer-focused initiatives,

have you used words such as "partner" and "adviser" instead of "work for" or "serve"?

❑ Have you checked for consistency with previously published messages?

❑ Have you identified where synergies exist across projects, geographies, and business units and communicated this in your message? Have you reviewed your message for possible global implications?

❑ When disseminating information that will impact peoples' lives (for example, human resources policies) have you explained the rationale behind the change?

❑ Does your message identify future opportunities for partnership with customers and ways to add value?

CULTURE

❑ Does your message reinforce the company's shared values?

❑ Does your message applaud and identify high-performing teams, heroes, and risk-takers even if they failed or made mistakes?

❑ Does your message address difficult or sensitive subjects in an open, candid way that encourages people to make constructive suggestions and raise other concerns?

❑ Have you solicited feedback?

❑ If your message describes teamwork, are you using "we" language rather than "I" or "us and them"?

❑ Have you positioned your leaders as members of a team with a shared purpose?

❑ Does your message promote fun and celebrate successes?

BEHAVIOR

❑ *Does your message reinforce and demonstrate the desired strategic behaviors?*

❑ *Have you identified how individuals or teams exhibited the desired strategic behaviors in the situation/information/initiative you are communicating? If real examples do not exist, have you identified what the strategic behaviors would "look like" in that situation?*

❑ *When providing guidelines, have you checked the tone to make sure the message is nondirective and inclusive?*

❑ *Have you encouraged and recognized the sharing, challenging, and development of ideas of global teams?*

❑ *Have you addressed how the message affects your employees, your internal customers, and/or the external customers?*

❑ *Have you identified the actions/learnings you would like the audience to take/gain as a result of your message now or in the future?*

❑ *If you are responding to a question/concern/suggestion, are you writing from the perspective of "what's right/smart" about what the other person has stated?*

❑ *When you are unsure about the underlying tone of a message and the behaviors you are reinforcing, have you found someone to review your draft and give you open and honest feedback?*

Note: Checklist created by Nextera's Bronwyn Poole and Caroline Chubb.

7

Celebrate Heroes

To be a hero, create and celebrate heroes.

The final leg on the eLeader's journey is the process of identifying, honoring, rewarding, and creating heroes within the organization. Heroes can be individuals, teams, or departments.

It's an old-fashioned idea, but a simple thing that makes business sense. By celebrating heroes, you accomplish three strategic tasks:

- You help keep the best and brightest with your organization by acknowledging their value to the organization.
- You reinforce desired behaviors throughout your company by giving your workforce real-life examples to follow.
- And you begin the process of finding successors for your top leadership team—because your best future leaders will be among the company's heroes.

Remember the 20/60/20 rule? An organization's workforce typically is divided into three sections: the top 20%, middle 60%, and bottom 20%. The top 20% of your workforce is the first group from which you will cull your heroes.

The top 20% is the group of high-performing employees who frequently work behind the scenes, against the rules, and undercover to achieve the performance they covet. They are willing to break the rules if they must. And the middle 60% of your workforce is a little afraid of them.

The middle 60% is convinced, down deep, that the top 20% who get the job done by breaking the rules are not only the troublemakers but are most likely to be fired—though that's rarely the case.

The eLeader's job is to bring those top-performing heroes into the spotlight. Tell their stories. Publicly celebrate the approach they take and the results they achieve.

Only then, when the top 20% "troublemakers" have been turned into public heroes, will the middle 60% truly understand that these high performers are not in trouble, and most certainly are not going to be fired. Instead, these are people whose successful, business-building behaviors the middle 60% should emulate.

Making the top 20% into organizational heroes is an extremely effective way to motivate the middle 60%. I call this the "Be Like Mike Syndrome."

Remember the Gatorade commercial from the early 1990s that featured Michael Jordan shooting hoops with kids at a playground basketball court? As the theme song played, "Like Mike—if I could be like Mike," the kids watched Jordan with worshipful eyes and tried to imitate his smooth moves. Each youngster, it was clear, wanted to be as smart, talented, self-confident, and famous as the basketball star—the ultimate top 20% performer. And if drinking Gatorade and wearing Nike shoes would help them achieve his level of success—well, they would do it.

Your employees are motivated by the same desires that motivated Jordan's playmates: They want to be heroes. They want to be appreciated and respected. They want to be honored for their work and have their stories seen in the company newsletter or video newsmagazine. They want their names mentioned in the same breath as your company's leaders.

Of course, the heroes in your organization won't be as glamorous as Michael Jordan. Few of us are. But if you create a plan to find and honor everyday, real-life heroes—at all levels of your organization—you will enlist valuable support for your transition to the New Economy.

The concept of celebrating heroes is nothing new. It's not as dramatic as speaking the unspeakable, making loud statements, or communicating irreverently. But here it's done a slightly different way by honoring unexpected people—the unsung heroes, the rulebreakers. And in an age where treating people well is both ethically and financially the right thing to do, old-fashioned concepts like this are more important than ever.

SBC: Little Bit of Soules

Bobby Soules is a hero at SBC. Fellow managers flock to see what he does. His employees love him. His supervisors extol his virtues.

Soules oversees a facility that in less than two years has increased productivity and decreased overtime costs. Under his leadership, the facility has cut its operations costs by more than $1 million, while virtually eliminating absenteeism.

Soules has become a master of best practices for SBC, the telecommunications company encompassing former Baby Bells Ameritech and Southwestern Bell. "He's become the poster child for us," says Dennis Harris, vice-president of human resources.

The secret of Soules's success is based in large part on creating and celebrating heroes.

In late 1997 Soules, a thirty-year company veteran, took over as area manager–facility assignment for one of SBC's mechanized loop assignment centers. The facility is essentially a center handling record-keeping and assignments for SBC's northern Texas market area.

When Soules arrived, it was a facility in trouble: It was posting high absenteeism, low productivity, high overtime costs, and overall high costs, compared to similar operations.

Soules immediately diagnosed a key problem: The center's one hundred employees felt they had little input into the business. "There were charts and graphs hanging up on the walls, for instance. But if you asked what they were, the people would say, 'You'll have to ask my boss,'" Soules remembers. "Managers did not know how to relinquish control."

In addition, Soules had been advised that a lot of the center's workers were stressed to the point of burnout.

He went to the union leadership to get their input. "They

said people didn't feel appreciated and valued, and there were a lot of things being done the wrong way," he says.

Soules then did a crazy thing: He asked those union leaders what they thought could be done to make the center a better workplace. When they told him that people wanted more input into their jobs, he decided to facilitate a series of meetings with each employee group.

And he did that crazy thing again: He asked the employees what they thought could make the center run better. They pointed to data that was being filed but never used and time-consuming paperwork that no one needed.

On the spot, Soules and his groups began eliminating archaic practices and meaningless paperwork. "Immediately, they began to like what was going on," he says.

Then he set up a series of business plan meetings: sessions where employees could air problems and resolve them together, then as a group set "milestones" for the coming year. The meetings included only the people actually doing the work; managers were not invited. Soules was present merely to facilitate.

He'd keep everyone posted on progress, and when the group reached one of its milestones, he'd make a big deal out of it, with a celebration. In 1999, his team celebrated seventeen milestones.

"As successes have come, I try to reinforce more and more that it's been their decisions or plans that led to the success—and I tell them how much I appreciate them," he says.

In addition to celebrating milestones, Soules made sure to leave his office two or three times a day and walk around the center. "I'll look the staff in the eye and ask how things are going and thank them for their work. And if I get a letter or email of commendation on someone's work, I'll go tell them about it."

In place of the useless charts and graphs that used to hang on the wall, Soules began posting success stories: photos of employees, with a caption explaining what results they had accomplished.

He also set up a "recognition committee" that celebrates people in a variety of ways. The committee had treats to celebrate the office moms and dads for Mother's Day and Father's Day. They filled up Easter baskets for local nursing homes.

Soules knew he was succeeding when a union job steward said to him, "You're making people feel important. And when people feel important, everything else falls into place."

His corporate boss, Dennis Harris, says, "As the trust grew, the dialogue grew. Bobby created an environment where the employees began to see that he cared about them as individuals, not as mere tools."

What Soules now finds is that "I can go out and ask folks to do anything for me and they'll do it. And vice versa."

But what he and SBC also have found is that treating people well and celebrating successes has translated into business success. Soules's techniques helped reduce one critical SBC productivity measurement from 13.9 percent per one hundred orders to 5.7 percent per one hundred orders—the lowest number in the company. The savings on that translated to $1.2 million for SBC. And

Soules did it with three fewer employees than when he took the post.

Overtime has dropped since Soules arrived. Absenteeism is down 95 percent.

And his group is receiving strong feedback from the customers it serves. "The product is better," they'd say. "Your people are so cordial and helpful. We wish all support groups were like this."

SBC has brought key executives and managers of other facilities down to tour Soules's happy Texas workplace. He now is sharing his ideas about creating and celebrating heroes with the rest of the company—giving him a chance to make other managers heroes too.

For Soules, it all comes down to attitude. "We work a lot on the skill sets of people but we don't work equally as hard on the attitude," he says. "You can take the best-trained person in the world and put them on the most up-to-date computer—but if his attitude is not good, his performance is going to reflect it.

"I've always believed that skill *plus* attitude equals performance."

That equation is working well for SBC.

Identify Them

You cannot celebrate heroes until you know who they are.

You may be able to sit down and immediately tick off a dozen names of likely candidates. These are probably well-known leaders within your organization—members of the top 20%, but those whose stories have been heard before. They likely are at the top of your organization already.

You need to push beyond that first set of names and dig to find the untold stories. The heroes in your company are those people who are implementing your strategy and getting results—at all levels of the organization.

You need to create a mechanism to identify heroes—and there are many possible ways to do so.

Internal communications: Use videos, newsletters, recognition walls, emails to spread the word. Create an intranet database of success stories.

When you have a kickoff meeting for your loud statement of change, think about creating a videotape celebrating heroes. Find the rulebreakers, the employees who have great stories to tell—the unsung heroes, the people behind the scenes, the unexpected. What we typically find is that the first video contains fairly predictable names and people higher up in the organization. But once everyone in the company sees that first tape, they get the idea; they know what we're looking for and start passing names on to us. The companies that do a second or third or fourth video celebrating heroes find the stories they get are richer, deeper, and push further into the organization.

Site reporters: For the purposes of a video newsmagazine or a company newsletter, you can create a team of "reporters" around the organization whose job it is to look for good stories and potential heroes.

Nextera has developed a course called Site Reporter Training. We recruit volunteers from the company, who assemble for a three-hour class taught by a real news reporter. The new "reporters" are given the criteria for a good story; we explain the kinds of behaviors we're looking for. They are taught how to investigate a story—how to ask the right questions to find people who are demonstrating the right behaviors. We give them reporters' notebooks and badges, and forms to fill out and send back when they find a lead.

Identifying a potential story is all we ask of them: A writer or producer will call to interview the hero candidate, and put the story together.

At GATX Terminals, our reporters were office managers in the field. At other companies, they might be secretaries, call center employees, or communications or public relations people.

Change Champions: Another possible mechanism is a Change Champion Team. Especially when Nextera is working with larger clients, we try to identify members of the top 20% across the company, in all offices around the world, who meet a set of criteria. Sometimes passing out the criteria to local managers will help them identify their high performers.

Typically, Change Champions are those who:

- Others rely on and go to for information
- Are well respected by everyone—peers, subordinates, and bosses alike
- Are flexible and willing to break the rules to achieve business results
- Instinctively respect other people
- Are persistent and positive even in uncertain situations
- Are enthused about the learning opportunities during the change process

Once we have identified a team of Change Champions, we try to gather them together in a single place to meet and share concerns and ideas. We also give them their mission: to figure out ways to reinforce the new behaviors and support the change process where they live. They keep the momentum of your loud statement of change going through the company.

At a global professional services firm we identified Change Champions from twenty-eight different countries to ensure that cultural sensitivities would be taken into account to reinforce the company's loud statement of change.

It's the Change Champions' job, for instance, to show that great video you made of the big meeting only managers could attend. They may have local town hall meetings. They may conduct their own training sessions or information forums on the new behaviors.

They should continue meeting as a peer group as well, to exchange ideas and techniques. They can brainstorm on contests, celebrations, and any other types of activities to reinforce the new behaviors in their local offices.

The Change Champions are heroes and should be recognized as such. They very likely are the crème de la crème— the top 20% of your top 20%. But you can use them to find other heroes. They have their ears to the ground. They're smart and know their departments or offices well. They can help identify heroes in corners of your organization.

Key communicators: You also can make your top managers responsible for finding heroes within their own parts of the company. During your key communicator training, when you are explaining and identifying the new behaviors sought by the organization, make sure these leaders understand the importance of watching for and rewarding these behaviors throughout the organization.

Honor Them

What makes an organization live and a new environment thrive is storytelling.

Once you know who they are, you need to share the stories of your company's heroes—as publicly and with as much fanfare as possible.

Every time you hold a meeting or a town hall session you should use the opportunity to tell a story about some real person who is living the organization's new behavior and implementing the new strategy. Have them stand up and be recognized. Feature them in newsletters or video newsmagazines, or on your intranet. Make sure everyone knows that these are the people who are doing the right things.

If these people have been working undercover to achieve their goals, this public recognition is vindicating for them: They don't necessarily need the praise, but it makes them feel good. But you really are identifying them publicly not for their sake, but for the others in the audience.

It's one thing to talk about new behaviors and strategies in the abstract. Putting a face on it makes it real for your employees, particularly the movable middle 60%. It makes it possible for them to say, "Hey, I could do that, too!"

Some of you will have to fight old cultural rules that frown upon public recognition of individuals. Luckily, many of your best stories will come from team efforts. But don't let that old culture mentality stop you from honoring worthy performance in an appropriate way.

The only important thing is that when you tell the stories of your heroes' successes, you tell the full and honest stories. People will benefit only if you tell the hard-fought battle story, not the spin. Each of these heroes encountered problems, obstacles, politics, setbacks. To be a real learning experience for everyone else, the retelling of the hero's story must share both the ups and downs, explaining what it really required to get the job done.

Here are real-life examples of how companies have honored their heroes:

Ernst & Young: If you set it up correctly, honoring heroes can become a continuing practice at your company.

The goal of 1999's "People Add Value" campaign, sponsored by the Lake Michigan region of Ernst &Young, was to show the company's employees that their efforts were appreciated. As mentioned earlier, the company sent out a videotape and then hosted a big bash at Chicago's House of Blues club during the middle of tax season, to prove that people mattered more than the work—that their bosses appreciated their efforts.

But the interesting twist was a complementary program called "Catch a Star." Not only did E&Y want its employees to know that the bosses appreciated their work, but they wanted employees to begin visibly appreciating each other more. So "Catch a Star" asked E&Yers to "catch" a fellow employee performing the behaviors needed to stay competitive, doing something great: taking risks, stepping out of the comfort zone, mentoring others, communicating well, supporting teamwork, or just being a friend.

The company printed bright yellow cardboard stars with room on the back to fill in a fellow employee's name and explain the good behavior.

To kick off the "Catch a Star" program, the company decided that to get into the House of Blues party, each E&Y employee had to bring at least one completed star.

The party organizers set aside one wall of the room and brought along twenty-five hundred pins to hang the stars. They were flabbergasted when they ran out of pins. The eleven hundred people attending the party had brought more than twenty-five hundred stars.

Needless to say, "Catch a Star" has been a big hit for E&Y. It's helped the company recognize its heroes and has fostered a spirit of teamwork. To this day, says Ray McGowan, partner–director of human resources, his department receives more than four hundred stars each month—and uses the stories to continue celebrating heroic behavior.

GATX Terminals: Finding and recognizing heroes can be critical during times of struggle.

When the old-line industrial company GATX Terminals was experiencing a time of industry change and upheaval, it created a newsletter and did a year-end video newsmagazine to honor its heroes. It was critical for GATX employees both because of the concern about what was happening at the corporate level and because employees at a given terminal had very little opportunity to communicate with those at the other terminals.

GATX trained office staffers as site reporters; they found stories about people who were being flexible, creative, and risk-takers. "The newsletter was full of hero stories, about people who were making a difference," says Teri Schram, who headed internal communications. "It was a huge success; everyone read it.

"In the midst of a very difficult year, it was important for us to celebrate our very big successes."

ABN AMRO NA: Creating a way to applaud your heroes can be vital when your organization is spread far and wide.

The North American division of this global financial institution has created a series of video newsmagazines called "Connections on the Air." The second edition, for instance, released in early 2000, featured stories of three different teams of employees. Each team was successfully living the new behaviors of teamwork, collaboration, and knowledge sharing needed to support the company's new strategic plan.

The video communication is critical for ABN AMRO, whose eighteen thousand employees are located in hundreds of offices and bank branches across North America. It gives the company's leadership a chance to reach employees who might never hear these stories and have a chance to learn from them.

Large energy company: You don't have to spend any money to honor your heroes.

At the kickoff meeting for its change initiative, the leader of this company wanted to honor some unrecognized heroes. He had identified people who were doing things right and achieving results. This company had a cumbersome culture, and these heroes were finding ways around it to succeed.

So after his speech, the leader left the podium and began telling stories. For each hero, he told the story of that person's success, then walked off the stage to shake the hero's hand and put an arm around his shoulder. It was a touching moment; one of the recognized heroes was moved to the point of tears.

In one story, a young man needed high-level approval to seal a deal. He had gone through the official chain of command without success. Finally he decided to wait in the parking lot until the leader whose signature he needed appeared. He made his case; the leader, admiring his tenacity and willingness to get the job done, broke the rules and went straight to the top to get the needed approval. The deal was made. And the young man was honored in front of everyone for his push to get what the company needed.

It was particularly effective because such a visible expression of thanks and emotion went against that culture's rules.

MSI Strategic Communications: One of the most important times to honor your heroes is when they leave.

MSI last year won an Emmy Award for a drug-abuse documentary. Partly on the basis of that documentary, a young staffer who had been a key member of the documentary team won a fellowship in film studies from Stanford University and decided to leave MSI.

When MSI president Susan Silk had to say goodbye to this star performer, she did the right thing. She composed an email to her staff and clients. In part, it read: "Our company challenges talented people to grow. We know that our staffers want new projects to work on and new skills to build upon. We try to provide an atmosphere where ideas are rewarded, where progress is supported, and where change is expected. It's great—except when you have to say, 'Congratulations & we'll miss you.' Because it is great to know that we have played a small part in helping Kristin form her dreams and make them into reality, but it is still sad to say, 'So long.'"

Speaking later about the incident, Silk says, "It was important for our employees to know how proud we are of their accomplishments, and how proud we are that we can create a platform from which they can accomplish these kinds of things."

Understand that as you train people and teach them new skills, you are making them more marketable. But that is part of your success. If you are a company providing good skills to people and offering a learning environment, you will have an easier time recruiting and retaining people. But in the process, you will lose some people. That is part of today's employee value proposition.

When a valued staffer leaves, use the opportunity to tell your employees: This is an environment where people learn things. Some of you learn from us and then are celebrated for your success with us. Some of you learn and are celebrated when you leave. But you are heroes nonetheless.

Reward Them

In addition to giving them public recognition for their achievements, you should create some visible signs of reward for your heroes.

That can be a financial reward. Some companies give a one-time special recognition award or bonus on some sort of regular basis (monthly, six times a year, twice a year, or annually). Other newer companies give additional stock options, for instance, to employees they specifically want to keep, or when they promote a hero. But money does not have to be the only incentive.

People—the middle 60% in particular—love plaques, trophies, certificates. When Sibson does a change effort, we try to brand the change with a theme and then tie any rewards into that theme.

AMFM's effort, for instance, was tagged "Bowling Over the Competition," and the company leaders planned to give out inscribed bowling pins to employees who offered excellent examples of the desired new behavior.

Make the reward sincere; don't choose the obvious employees, the goody-two-shoes or the teacher's pets. But at the same time, as much as you can, make the awards fun and even campy, rather than serious and hokey. Keeping the irreverent spirit alive in your rewards will appeal particularly to your Generation X and Y employees.

Dave Tolmie, CEO of yesmail.com, laughs about his "Just Dew It" award. At the company's first meeting, he began recognizing people for their hard work and success. But he had nothing to give them. In true start-up fashion, someone grabbed a can of Mountain Dew and handed it to Tolmie, who used it as a cigar band might be used as a substitute for a real wedding ring.

But everyone liked the idea, and the can of Mountain Dew became institutionalized. Now the company puts a label on each can before Tolmie gives it out.

"It's recognition for certain performance: extra effort, demonstrating a team mentality," Tolmie says.

The soft drink can serves as a symbol of how well people have done—of their extraordinary efforts. It serves as a token of how much their efforts are appreciated by their leaders and peers. And it is that appreciation, not the reward itself, that means the most to your organization's heroes.

Create Them

If you are doing it right, through the process of identifying and honoring heroes, you will be creating new heroes.

First, you're telling the movable middle 60% of your work-force how they, too, can become stars by giving them real-life examples to emulate. At the same time, the possibility of be-ing recognized as a hero—and the rewards it brings—will make them more eager to shoot for the stars.

Keep a mechanism like the Change Champions team alive, and keep adding new people to it when you find them. Being named a Change Champion—or whatever heroic des-ignation you might choose—is an honor and should be per-ceived as such.

Continue digging for the stories of individual employees

and teams who are making a difference at your company—those people who are flourishing in the new environment you have nurtured, and who are demonstrating the best new behavior to achieve strategic goals.

A strategy is nothing but words on paper. On its own, it will never get you where you want to go. The rubber hits the road when your employees bring that strategy to life and implement it day in and day out using the new behaviors that get the job done.

These heroes are the people who will ultimately make you, the eLeader, a hero too.

In the New Economy, adding value to the customer will come from the resources inside your employees' brains. To create an environment that will thrive in the twenty-first century, you must show people how to access that creativity, how to think through problems, how to address obstacles.

The stories of their successes will become the symbols of your new environment. And those stories will be about flexibility. They will demonstrate how people do what's needed today, how they turn on a dime, how they have learned how to change paths when necessary.

In the past, success stories tended to be about people who followed the rules to get the job done. From those stories came traditions, templates, and formulas.

Today, however, there are no templates and certainly no formulas: There are only critical thinking skills. There are no traditions, merely immediate solutions.

In celebrating people's ability to move fast, adjust quickly, and turn on a dime, you are celebrating their thinking skills. It is that process that you want to duplicate: People using their brainpower and analytical skills and resourcefulness to find ways to compete today—using the limited information they have and finding the best solution they can—in an environment where there are no clear paths to success.

That is heroic behavior for the New Economy.

Conclusion

ELEADERSHIP IS A JOURNEY. A journey to live out your dreams. A journey to change the world from the inside out.

It's about the people you met along the way.

It's about people like Kim Woods. Perhaps to your surprise, Kim was my student at DePaul University. An eager student, she called me when the class was over; she wanted me to come to her company, ABN AMRO, and pitch a cultural assessment. ABN AMRO is the thirteenth-largest bank in the world, and I knew it would be a big contract—and I knew there wasn't a prayer that my Gen Xer, Kim, would be able to give us that kind of contract. But I went anyway because I wanted to teach her something. Guess what? Within three weeks, we got the proposal and she had gotten us an appointment with Harry Tempest, the chairman of ABN AMRO NA. That's eLeadership—starting with a Gen Xer who partnered with a seasoned veteran to do what was best for the business.

It's about people like Oakleigh Thorne, who looked into the camera and told his employees at CCH that the ship wasn't going down on his watch. Not only did the ship not go down, but Oakleigh took a ninety-year-old book publishing company with a stock value of fourteen dollars and reengineered it into a software company—and ended up selling it for fifty-seven dollars a share only three years later. It's about the man at the print shop in Florida who had worked at CCH his whole life, and invested his 401K monies in CCH stock. He informed me that Oakleigh hadn't let him down: On that day of the sale, this man had become a millionaire.

It's about people like Jimmy de Castro, who had to look his buddies in the eye and let them go because it was the right thing for everyone—including them. In this age of merger and transition, he did such a good job creating a new team that when AMFM went through an inevitable merger with Clear Channel Communications, many of Jimmy's well-chosen leaders ended up in great positions running radio station groups in the country's biggest markets.

It's about people like Ken Lawson. Ken was one of the most proactive, courageous leaders I'd ever met. He made the decision to change his company when it was number one in its industry with an 80 percent market share. But he knew they couldn't sustain the growth. He looked me right in the eye and said, "I can't change my behavior, but I can keep my mouth shut." That was the most courageous thing I'd ever seen someone do. I went to Ken's retirement party and saw his dream come true: He passed the torch to the next generation, knowing that his company was in great shape and would live on past his reign.

It's about people like Andy Rosenfield from Unext.com. I was at a meeting where people were describing their leader and how much they loved working for him, and I knew this was someone I had to get to know. It was Andy. Although the story is not done yet, I believe Andy is going to realize his dream to democratize education and get that educational experience for people all over the world.

It's about people like Lawrence Baxter, who came out of academia and understood that the Socratic method that he'd used to teach was the same method he could use to overcome the obstacles in a traditional bank—in his effort to build an electronic bank and achieve goals everyone said couldn't be met.

It's about people like Carl Russo, who built a company from the ground up. He focused on the environment; he wanted to permit creativity to flourish, and wanted the workforce to feel like a family. Not only did he accomplish that, but that great environment proved to be good business too. He sold that business, Cerent Corp., to the quintessential eLeader, Cisco Systems, for $7 billion.

It's about attending an Illinois technology conference last year and hearing fifteen speakers. Two of them stood out: Dave Tolmie of yesmail.com and Brad Keywell of Starbelly.com. When I saw them at the microphone I knew they were eLeaders of tomorrow. They were people who wanted to make a difference. Not only did they want to change the world by creating new channels of distribution, but they wanted to break all the rules of the past and create an environment where ideas would thrive.

Last but not least, it's about the Bobby Souleses of the world, who instinctively do right by people—who then in turn do the right things for their companies.

These are the legacies of eLeaders—those people with guts and vision, people who want to change the world from the inside out. They are willing to take risks and willing to make decisions with less-than-complete information. Most important, these are people who want to do the right thing— the right thing in terms of building their businesses, the right thing in terms of creating an environment that people are proud to be a part of.

Index